GREAT SHOTS

GREAT SHOTS

ROBERT SOMMERS
and
CAL BROWN

CHARTWELL
BOOKS, INC.

First published in Great Britain in 1989
by Anaya Publishers Ltd. 49 Neal Street, London WC211 9PJ

This edition published by Chartwell Books, Inc., a division of
Book Sales, Inc., 110 Enterprise Avenue, Secausus, New Jersey 07094

Additional text: Norman Dabell
Editor: Christopher Plumridge
Picture Researches: Andrea Stern, Janet Seagle
Design: Peartree Design Associates

The Publishers wish to thank David Mead, who encouraged
them to commission this book.

The stories of Gene Sarazen's double-eagle at the US Masters in 1935 and
Gary Player's 9-iron shot at the 1972 US PGA Championship are updated
versions of articles that appeared originally in *Golf Digest (U.S.A.)
Magazine*. We gratefully acknowledge *Golf Digest's* permission to reprint
excerpts from its issues of April 1970 (Sarazen) and October 1972 (Player)

ISBN 1-55521-554-8

Typeset by Tradespools, Frome, Somerset
Colour origination by Marfil, S. L. (Madrid)
Printed in Spain by Edime, S. A. (Madrid)
D. L. M-1.066-1990

CONTENTS

INTRODUCTION

In the course of researching this book, we asked Ben Hogan "What was the best shot, or best shots, anyone played *against* you?"

A man of very few words, who speaks only after serious study, Hogan hesitated not at all.

"All of them," he groaned. "Every damned one."

Hogan's melancholy response might wring a smile from those who struggled against him and believe they suffered enough from Hogan's own great shots.

Collect any three golfers and it's a fair guess they couldn't agree on the game's greatest shots. The selection is too subjective; deciding which shots to include is easier than choosing which to exclude.

On these matters, we were as vulnerable to prejudice as the next man, and we feel obliged to explain how the shots were chosen. We do not offer our selections as a definitive list of the 50 greatest shots ever played, but rather we've assembled what we consider 50 *great* shots we believe are likely to be mentioned when golfers talk about the game's memorable or dramatic strokes.

The home of golf: the Royal and Ancient Golf Club of St Andrews.

Many more than these have been played – indeed, we considered 300 for this collection.

That the stroke was brilliantly played mattered, of course, but when it was played and under what circumstances mattered more; it was more important that it was played on the great occasion. Those that seem most memorable to us, and the most admirable for their display of nerve and skill, are those played under the greatest emotional strain, or pressure, which tends to happen most often in the six major Championships – the United States and British Open and Amateur Championships, the Masters Tournament and the United States PGA Championship.

We believe we have our facts straight. We went to some lengths to talk with each of the subjects still living, hoping we could project their own emotions and reactions.

As a species, golfers don't pay much attention to the shots their rivals play. Hogan is the classic example. Paired with him in the Masters Tournament some years ago, Claude Harmon scored a hole in one on the perplexing 12th hole at Augusta National. Harmon walked on to the green and, with the crowd still cheering, picked his ball from the cup. Hogan then holed a difficult breaking putt for a birdie two.

They strode together to the 13th, where Hogan surprised Harmon by stepping on to the tee, preparing to drive first. As he teed up his ball, Hogan shook his head and said, "You know, Claude, that's the first time I've ever birdied that hole." Stunned, Harmon sputtered, "But Ben, I have the honor; I made a one." Remember, Hogan and Harmon were friends.

That incident reminds us that a great shot isn't always given the recognition it deserves. Not all of them have been played in winning causes, but nevertheless they've been delivered when they were needed, under the most trying conditions. Some of them have been included; many haven't.

The shots we have chosen are arranged in three groups according to what we considered their unusual quality. The first section, **Making History**, includes those shots that have had a dramatic impact on the game, shots most of us would agree were indeed historic because of the circumstances. In the second part, **Turning The Tide**, we have grouped together those shots we considered decisive and that defined a turning point in the direction of a tournament. Our third category, **Seizing The Moment**, brings together shots of extraordinary merit played at a critical, although not always winning, moment.

Which of these 50 shots do we consider the greatest? Each of us makes his own choice. It depends on how you look at the game, doesn't it? Bernard Darwin saw Jess Sweetser and Bobby Jones play a semi-final match for the 1922 US Amateur Championship at The Country Club, the storied ground near Boston, Massachusetts, where Francis Ouimet, the young amateur, had out-scored Harry Vardon and Ted Ray in the US Open nine years earlier. Both Sweetser and Jones played extraordinary approaches to the 2nd green. Sweetser holed a 50-yard pitch for a two, and then Jones played a shot from an equal distance that landed on the front of the green and ran straight for the cup, stopping only six inches short. Writing about the incident, Darwin called these "the greatest little shots" he had ever seen.

Jones meant to hole his shot, and he nearly did. This was one of those sublime moments when a player's nerves match his resolve and his skill, and the result takes your breath away.

Those wonderful little shots aren't even included in this book. You see how it is, don't you?

Opposite, Tom Watson's stirring victory in the 1977 British Open came after an historic battle with Jack Nicklaus.

MAKING HISTORY

SANDY LYLE

7-iron to the 18th at Augusta in the 1988 US Masters

It has been put about that Sandy Lyle lacks a certain fire in his approach to the game, that his emotional threshold is rather lower than it might be. Lyle plods along, hits his shots, and pulls the ball from the hole with none of the obvious satisfaction, let alone elation, of many of his fellows.

There is a suggestion that his enormous talent might blossom if he were to go after things with greater enthusiasm, or at least with the murderous intent of a Hogan or a Nicklaus. His performance in the 1988 Masters Tournament suggests this is possibly a disservice to the man. It all came down to a single stroke on the final hole from a difficult spot that allowed for no error.

Lyle is a big, powerful man with an unorthodox swing that one hardly expects from the son of a golf professional. He whips the club round his back in an ungainly swirl, then drives the club forward with little fuss. Like Jones and Snead before him, although

no one would liken his muscular lunge to either man, Lyle takes the club rather more inside than modern theory recommends and then brings it through almost perfectly on line. This is a method that only the exceptionally gifted might want to try, but it produces an ideal swing plane that allows him to attack the ball from directly behind; thus at impact he wastes none of his considerable power. Most of us can scarcely appreciate what it means to hit a 1-iron 270 yards, as Lyle does routinely.

The Augusta National golf course invites power, perhaps too obviously, but it asks for even more in the way of judgment and composure. Lyle had played well in the early stages of the 1988 Masters. He led after two rounds and by the time the leaders had reached the final nine holes of the fourth round, Lyle had moved to eight under par and led by three strokes. Then, he stumbled. He bogeyed the 11th and double-

Sandy Lyle drives from the 18th at Augusta.

bogeyed the par-three 12th. Not for nothing have these holes come to be known as Amen Corner. At the 12th Lyle played boldly for the flagstick set on the right corner, the most dangerous side. It fell just short, and plunged into the pond in front of the green.

As the ripples spread, Lyle covered his face in dismay. He had now lost three strokes in two holes, bringing half a dozen players back into the hunt. These were Mark Calcavecchia, Fred Couples, Greg Norman, who had already finished with a stunning 64, and former Masters winners Craig Stadler, Bernhard Langer and Ben Crenshaw. Not many shrinking violets there. Calcavecchia was boldest and steadiest of all, finishing with 282, six under par.

Lyle had seemed shaky when he missed an easy birdie putt at the 15th, but then he drew even by dropping a long, slippery birdie putt on the 16th. He came to the final hole needing a four to tie, and a three to win.

The 18th is an uphill par-four that turns gently to the right. Two steeply-faced bunkers billow from the far side of the fairway where the hole turns, then the ground rises toward a pitching, two-level green. For most players, a drive with a touch of fade and then a middle iron.

Driving with his 1-iron, Lyle lashed his ball far up the hill, but, alas, straight. The ball bounded into the first of the fairway bunkers, 2 i6 yards from the tee.

Another grimace. The ball was sitting up nicely, but it had come to rest not two yards from the bunker's steep front bank. Lyle would have to play the next shot with that annoying lip staring directly at him.

The flagstick was on the lower front portion of the green, tucked behind a yawning bunker that is no friend to someone in Lyle's position. He was 148 yards from the hole. He chose a 7-iron and stepped resolutely into the pit. His swing barely grazed the sand, picking the ball cleanly, raising nothing more visible than a faint puff of dust. The ball flew high, straight over the flag, hit into the bank toward the rear of the green and nearly stopped. Slowly, ever so slowly, it rolled back down the slope to within eight feet of the hole.

A sharp cry of admiration arose for this brave and wonderful stroke, and then a stunning silence spread through the gallery as the import of the shot registered. Victory was a short putt away, and a straight one at that, one of the few Augusta National offers.

Clad all in light brown and wearing a white visor, Lyle stroked the ball confidently into the hole, finishing with a round of 71 and a total of 281, one better than Calcavecchia.

Lyle was the first player from Great Britain — and only the fourth foreign player — to win the Masters. He was typically restrained and phlegmatic after his victory. About all he would say of that extraordinary shot was that it felt good.

"I could tell by the feel of the club it was a good shot," he said. "I did the right thing for a change."

Indeed. He had come back from a patch of ruinous golf, gathered himself and then played a winning stroke with confidence and not a little daring. That would seem to be enough fire, visible or not, to get by on for a while.

C.B.

❧ I could tell by the feel of the club it was a good shot. I did the right thing for a change. ❧

Lyle recovers brilliantly from the sand to within 12 feet of the hole.

The putt is on its way.

The ball drops and Lyle is the first British winner of the US Masters.

Tom Watson and Jack Nicklaus

shots to the 18th at Turnberry in the 1977 British Open

Duel in the sun as Tom Watson and Jack Nicklaus fight for the 1977 British Open title in perhaps the finest finish in the Championship's history.

Golf has never been played at a higher level than on a warm and sunny July afternoon in 1977 at Turnberry, Scotland. Tom Watson was just reaching his peak as the game's leading player and Jack Nicklaus was still the most dangerous man in the game. A third British Open, a fourth US Open, a fifth US PGA Championship and a sixth Masters Tournament still lay ahead of him, and as the final day of this championship wore on, he was playing as if he might win this British Open as well.

Most of Watson's important victories were yet to come. He had won the British Open in 1975, defeating the Australian Jack Newton in a play-off at Carnoustie, and earlier in 1977 had won the Masters in another stirring confrontation with Nicklaus. He had been unjustly called a choker in his earlier years because he had had two weak finishes in US Opens, closing with 79 at

Winged Foot in 1974, falling five strokes behind Hale Irwin, and the very next year finishing with 78–77 at Medinah after starting 67–68. By now, though, he had erased those earlier unfortunate times and had grown into as dangerous a clutch player as anybody in the game.

This was the first British Open ever played at Turnberry. Even though its Ailsa course had been acknowledged to be of championship caliber, the Royal and Ancient Golf Club, which conducts the Championship, had been concerned that the road system might not be adequate. Before long it was clear the roads were fine.

July 1977 was unusually warm and the country had suffered through a drought the preceding year. Consequently, Turnberry became a fast-running course, playing much shorter than it might have, and the rough had curled over and died. Furthermore, only light

winds drifted in from the Irish Sea. Scores reflected the benign conditions. Eight men broke 70 in the first round and then Mark Hayes shot 63 in the second.

Watson and Nicklaus, meantime, had been playing nearly stroke for stroke. Both men opened with 68 and 70, and then raced around Turnberry in 65 in the third round. With 203 for 54 holes,

Jack Nicklaus is one stroke ahead with nine holes to play.

they stood three strokes ahead of Ben Crenshaw. Tommy Horton was next, at 209. It was clear this would be a struggle between Nicklaus and Watson, just as it had been at Augusta in April, but where Watson had played immediately ahead of Nicklaus then, this time they would be paired together for the showdown, the last men off the tee.

Early in the round it looked as if this would be Jack's turn to win. He birdied two of the first four holes, opening a three-stroke lead, but Watson fought back, picked up two strokes over the next three holes and turned for home trailing Jack by one stroke. Nicklaus had played the first nine in 33, Watson in 34.

Other than missing a couple of hole-able putts, Jack hadn't made a mistake, while Watson had made two, missing the 2nd and 9th greens, and taking bogeys.

As they swung around Turnberry's far turn, out by the lighthouse, their golf was of another world. One flawless shot followed another, as Watson applied pressure. Still Nicklaus held on, fighting off the best Watson could throw at him, clinging to his one-stroke edge through 14 tough, tense holes. Nicklaus was frustrated as well. He stood 3 under par for the round, 10 under for 68 holes, and still he couldn't shake loose from Watson.

Then suddenly the pressure eased. Playing first on the 15th, a 209-yard par three slightly downwind, Watson made his third mistake, pulling his 4-iron toward a greenside bunker. His ball barely cleared the trap, ran about three yards past and rolled on to a grassy lie on a downslope at least 20 yards from the hole. Seeing Watson in trouble, Nicklaus played a safer shot, on to the right center of the green, leaving him with two putts for a certain three.

Watson, though, was never out of a hole. Taking his putter, he rapped his ball smartly down the slope and on to

Nicklaus lines up a putt, always trying to keep his lead.

have a chance at tying Watson and forcing a play-off.

Driving first, Tom played a 1-iron and strung his shot down the center of the fairway. Nicklaus, however, couldn't afford to waste distance, and so chose to play his driver. He drew the club back in that high arc and swung into the ball with all his immense power, but he blocked it out. Instead of travelling toward the right-to-left bend in the fairway, his ball shot off to the right, settling into the prickly gorse. He was in serious trouble now, for Tom would almost surely make his four, and to have any chance at all Jack needed a three.

Watson, of course, knew of Jack's unbending will and he realized Nicklaus would not give up. He stood 4 under par for the round, 11 under for 71 holes, and even though he was tearing Turnberry apart, he realized he couldn't relax the pressure. With no less a fighting spirit than Jack's, Tom drew out his 7-iron, swung into the shot with his usual quick motion and rifled his ball straight at the flagstick. It hung in the clear, blue sky, then dropped gently on to the green no more than three feet from the cup. A glorious shot. Now Nicklaus.

When he reached his ball, Jack found it among the bushes, but lying clear enough to him to play a shot. He had to make a choice. He could play safely back to the fairway, pitch on and hope to save a par, which would win him nothing, or he could risk going for the green, which might cost him more than one stroke.

Second place was of no interest, of course. Besides, both he and Watson were so far ahead – Hubert Green had finished at 279, only one under par – there was no danger of his dropping into third place. Jack truly had no choice to make; he had to go for it. There was still the chance Watson would miss his putt, and if Jack pulled

the green. It ran straight for the cup, hit the flagstick and dived into the hole. A birdie two. Nicklaus missed his birdie and now they were tied, with three holes to play.

Both men made their par fours on the 16th, but then Watson hit a gorgeous 3-iron on to the 17th green, the last of the par fives, and made still another birdie, his sixth of the day. Nicklaus missed the green with his second, pitched on nicely, but missed another shortish putt.

Jack had dropped a stroke behind and now he needed a birdie on the 18th to off this shot, he might birdie and force a play-off.

Taking his stance as best he could, knowing his hands would rip into those barbs sticking from the gorse, he played an 8-iron and, without flinching, hit the ball about as hard as he could. No one can say how he managed, but he hit that

Tom Watson takes infinite care on his putts too, and in the end is triumphant.

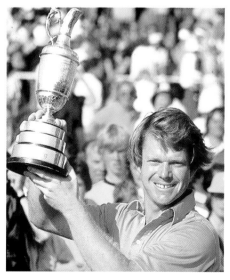

ball right on to the front right corner of the green, 30 to 35 feet from the cup. It was a magnificent shot, played under enormous pressure. It was more than that, though. This shot gave us all an insight into the man's unyielding will. Nicklaus would give nothing away.

Reaching the green, Watson walked to his ball and marked it. Nicklaus would putt first. Knowing that Jack would fight to the end, Watson sensed he would hole his putt and that he had better prepare himself for his three-footer.

Just as Watson had foreseen, Nicklaus ran it in. A birdie where a bogey had seemed likely and 66 for the round, 269 for the 72 holes, seven strokes under the previous record. Now it was up to Watson.

Tom's ball lay just about as far from the cup as Doug Sanders's had on the 18th at the Old Course at St Andrews, in 1970 in his play-off with Nicklaus. Sanders had missed. There would be no missed putt here. Fighting off the tension, Watson stroked his ball smoothly and it ran into the hole. A 65, one stroke better than Nicklaus, and a new 72-hole record of 268. He had won the British Open for a second time.

No one could remember a more stirring finish in championship golf, the two greatest golfers of the age matching shots, fighting stroke for stroke over a superb golf course with one of the world's four most important titles in the balance. Tied for the lead after the first two rounds, Nicklaus had played the last 36 holes in 65–66, for 131, but that wasn't good enough. Watson had played those last 36 holes in 65–65, for 130, and he had done it walking stride for stride with Nicklaus.

This was truly a Championship for the ages, and those two shots into the final green examples of grace and strength under fire.

R.S.

GENE SARAZEN

*4-wood double-eagle to the 15th at Augusta
in the 1935 US Masters*

"When the wand touches him, Gene Sarazen is likely to win in a great finish; the boldness of his play leaves no middle ground." Bobby Jones wrote that in 1932. Three years later Jones would stand on the golf course he built in Augusta, Georgia, and watch Sarazen fire "the shot heard round the world."

Gene Sarazen in top form in 1935 ...

Sarazen holed a 4-wood second shot on the par five 15th at Augusta National and went on to win the second Masters Tournament ever played. If not the greatest, that shot is certainly the most famous single stroke in the history of American golf. Sarazen's double-eagle dramatized, as no other shot had done, that rare achievement, scoring three under par on a given hole.

By the time Sarazen reached the 15th tee, the 1935 Masters seemed to be over, with Craig Wood the certain winner after he had birdied the final hole and posted a score of 282. Sarazen would have to birdie three holes to tie. The 15th measured 485 yards, a straightaway hole with a pond in front of the green. It has been lengthened since, to 520 yards, and the pond broadened from its original width of 30 feet to about 50 feet, but even then, a player thought twice before going for the green with his second shot. The turf was harder then than it is now, and Sarazen's drive, aided by a slight draw, rolled to a stop in the center of the fairway about 255 yards from the tee.

No more than 25 people huddled near the green on that blustery April afternoon; most of the gallery had flocked to the 18th to watch Wood. "I've met about 20,000 people who claim they saw the shot," Sarazen said. Two who did were Walter Hagen, who was paired with Gene, and Bobby Jones, who was perched on one of the large mounds between the 15th and 17th fairways.

It was a little past 5.30 in the afternoon. A roar from the 18th green, whipped by a cold gust of wind, reached them, followed moments later by the news of Wood's birdie. As Sarazen reached his ball, Hagen shook his head and called over: "Well, that's that," implying the Tournament was all over now.

"Oh I don't know," Sarazen replied, "they might go in from anywhere."

The ball was sitting down in the grass. Sarazen turned to his caddie, an amiable, lanky man called Stovepipe: "I'm going for it," Sarazen announced. "What do I need?"

"Mister Gene," Stovepipe drawled, "you got to hit you a 3-wood if you wants to clear that water."

As Sarazen pondered the shot, Hagen hollered across, "Hey, hurry up, Gene, I got a date tonight."

"I don't want the 3-wood," Sarazen said finally, and pulled out the 4-wood.

He toed in the face, took his stance and swung. The ball rose about 40 feet, flew dead straight and landed a few inches short of the green. "I hit it pure," Gene said later. "All I was hoping to do was make a 4."

Jones watched as the ball skipped low on to the putting surface and ran toward the flagstick, set in the right rear, about 15 feet from the back edge. "My God," Jones thought, "he's going to have a chance at a 3." An instant later the ball rolled up and in. Later, the shot was paced off at 232 yards.

"The first thing I thought about," Sarazen said, "was what I would have to do on the last three holes to tie Wood. I felt no elation. It came too quick."

On the last three holes, Jones remembered that Gene left himself difficult putts for pars and made them all. "What impressed me most," Jones said, "was his absolute confidence. He walked right up and struck them solidly and quickly. Every one of them went into the center of the hole. Gene was one of those players who, when he got on a hot streak, charged around the course like a tiger."

After making the double-eagle, Sarazen never doubted he would tie Wood and then win the 36-hole play-off. The next day he shot 144 against Wood's 149.

A bridge was erected across the pond in 1955 and named for Sarazen. He is

... and still a strong player nearly fifty years later.

probably remembered as much for this stroke as for being the first to win the US Open, the British Open, the US PGA and the Masters during his career, for having won the US Open at 20 and for his remarkable longevity.

Not long ago he reminisced about the double-eagle from his home in Marco Island, Florida. "You know, that was a lucky shot. It meant so much at the time, but I'm almost getting tired of hearing about it."

Sarazen was never a man to look back on things, but if we can be sure of one thing, it is that whenever the subject turns to great shots, Sarazen's is the first to be mentioned.

C.B.

❧ You know, that was a lucky shot. It meant so much at the time, but I'm almost getting tired of hearing about it. ❧

BEN HOGAN

1-iron to the 18th at Merion in the 1950 US Open

Back view of the come-back: Hogan's approach to the 18th at Merion earns its place among golf's legendary shots.

Eight months after winning the 1948 US Open, Ben Hogan had been seriously injured in a car accident and hadn't been able to defend his Championship the following June. After months of recovery, he had returned to golf in January 1950 and surprised everyone by nearly winning the Los Angeles Open. He tied Sam Snead, but lost to him in a play-off.

Remarkable though this might have been, no one knew what to expect from Hogan in the Open, which was to be played at the Merion Golf Club, near Philadelphia. Nor could they guess if his battered legs could stand up under the punishment of the 36-hole double round of the last day.

After 54 holes, Hogan was only two strokes behind Lloyd Mangrum, the leader. George Fazio, the first man out in the afternoon, had finished with 287, which didn't seem low enough for a winning score until the leaders began losing strokes. Mangrum had been all over the place on the first nine, but had steadied himself, come home in 35 and matched Fazio's 287; Dutch Harrison had come in with 288, and Cary Middlecoff, the defending Champion, had shot 41 on the first nine and dropped from the hunt.

Paired with Middlecoff, Hogan had played steady, nearly flawless golf and, with 37 on the first nine, he had moved into the lead. He stood three strokes ahead after eleven holes, but now his legs began to throb and he could barely move them as he struggled through those last gruelling holes. He almost didn't finish. Driving from the 12th tee, his legs locked and he nearly fell. He stumbled to a friend, put a hand on his shoulder and said, "Let me lean on you. My God, I don't think I can finish."

But he kept on. He played a wonderful iron that drifted softly down about eight feet from the cup, but he three-putted. One stroke gone. Two routine pars, then he three-putted the 15th and lost the last stroke of his lead by bunkering his tee shot on the 17th, a very long par three.

He was level with Mangrum and Fazio now, with only the hard 18th to play, 448 yards long with a blind drive that had to carry 210 yards across an old stone quarry and over the crest of a hill to reach the fairway beyond. He must have a par four here to tie.

Hogan hit a fine straight drive to a level spot well over the brow of the hill. Now he faced a long shot into a difficult green. The hole was cut to the right rear; a bunker reached around the right front and the green ran uphill for a distance, then fell away. Too strong a shot would run off the back and into the gallery. He had played a 4-iron into this green in the morning, but he was very tired now and he would need much more club.

Hogan studied his lie and decided he had two options: if he needed a par, he would play a safe 1-iron on to the left front; if he needed a birdie, he would play a much more dangerous shot and try to cut a 4-wood on to the right rear.

There were no leader boards in those days; the players relied on word of mouth. Not sure of the situation, Hogan asked, "What's low?" Fred Corcoran, who ran the tour in those days, said, "287 is low." A par four would tie; Hogan played the 1-iron.

A solid ring of fans encircled the hole, from behind Hogan, along both sides of the fairway, and around and behind the green, standing quietly as he prepared himself for the shot. He went into his usual routine: feet set, a look at the hole, a waggle or two, then the quick backswing, powerful downthrust, exaggerated extension through the ball and the high, full, perfectly balanced finish. The ball streaked from the face of the club, climbed into the pale blue sky and settled just where he aimed it, on the left front of the green, 40 feet from the pin. Two putts and he had his par, had come back in 37, shot 74 and had tied Mangrum and Fazio at 287. The next day he shot 69, Mangrum 73, and Fazio 75 in the play-off.

Strangely, Hogan didn't see that 1-iron again until many years later. Between the time he played the shot and the time the clubs were put away for the night, the 1-iron disappeared, stolen from his bag. It turned up again, however, in 1983, although no one connected with its return wants to talk about it. Hogan kept it in his office for a long time, debating its authenticity. Finally deciding it was indeed his club, he had it regripped as it had been in 1950 and gave it to the USGA to be displayed in the Association's museum alongside his portrait.

The clubface is curious in one respect: it is worn away toward the heel, as if an especially gifted golfer had hit ball after ball in the same precise spot.

R.S.

Let me lean on you. My God, I don't think I can finish.

GARY PLAYER

9-iron to the 16th at Oakland Hills in the 1972 US PGA

Gary Player has found much in the game to give him pleasure, one would have thought, and yet he has often talked less about golf's satisfaction than its trials. There is an earnest, sombre tone to his performance, even when the great moments have arrived.

"Golf is a game of sorrows, not one of pleasures," Player said after he had won the 1972 US PGA Championship. He offered this sober appraisal despite a richly satisfying victory that came to him after one bold and dramatic stroke had rescued him from disaster.

The 16th at Oakland Hills: the trees on the right blocked Gary Player's second shot in 1972.

The tournament was played at Oakland Hills, near Detroit, one of America's most punishing courses. Player had not won a major Championship since 1968 and a newspaper had suggested he was no longer one of the mythical "Big Three" of professional golf, along with Arnold Palmer and Jack Nicklaus. This disturbed him. There were other sorrows waiting for him on the golf course, but Player was conditioned to these.

He led by three strokes heading into the final round on a drizzly, gray Sunday, but he bogeyed three of the first four holes, then missed two very short putts on the second nine he felt he should have made. Discouraged, he sliced his drive wildly on the 16th.

At that moment five others were still in position to win. Closing fast, Billy Casper had just birdied the 16th and 17th, Jim Jamieson and Tommy Aaron stood only a stroke behind Player and, to the general approval and astonishment of the galleries, 60-year-old Sam Snead was throwing a scare into everyone. He scorched round the first nine in 32 and had he not missed two rather short putts coming back, he would have finished a stroke behind the winner. As it was, he closed with 69 over one of the game's harshest tests.

Player trudged after his drive at the 16th, a dangerous par four that curls to the right around a lake and lofty weeping willow trees. A bogey or worse could cost him the tournament. He found his ball in the wet rough behind one of the willows, 150 yards from the green. To reach it he would have to loft the ball over the trees and clear the lake, whose waters lap the shoreline inches from the putting surface.

Player normally plays a 7-iron from 150 yards, but he knew it would not clear the trees. "I had to gamble I could hit the 9-iron hard enough to carry the water. I know one thing: I have finished second in five majors, and the only per-

The final putt drops and Player has a second US PGA title to his name.

son who knows it is my wife," he said.

He could not see the flag, so he aimed for a shooting stick someone had left sticking in the ground. Placing the ball well forward in his stance, he smashed through the long grass with everything he had. The ball soared high over the trees, hung for a long time in the gray overcast sky and then plugged into the green four feet from the hole.

It was one of the greatest pressure shots Player or anyone else had ever struck. After he holed his birdie putt, Gary's sorrows were over. He nursed his lead to the finish, his score of 281 bringing him the sixth of his nine major championships.

Many years later, Player recalled that stroke with something that resembled grim satisfaction, if not pleasure. "It was either do or die. Golf is a punishing game, and when you play it for a living, it punishes you every week. For every guy who's happy, there are 100 who are sad," he said.

So there you have it, punishment and sorrow. Evidently some men see the game for what it is.

C.B.

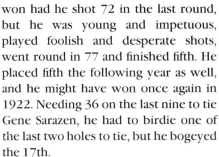

BOBBY JONES

mid-iron approach to the 18th at Inwood Country Club in the 1923 US Open

The classic finish of Bobby Jones's swing.

Bobby Jones had played in his first national championship in 1916, as a 14-year-old prodigy. He entered his first United States Open in 1920, when he was 18. He might have won had he shot 72 in the last round, but he was young and impetuous, played foolish and desperate shots, went round in 77 and finished fifth. He placed fifth the following year as well, and he might have won once again in 1922. Needing 36 on the last nine to tie Gene Sarazen, he had to birdie one of the last two holes to tie, but he bogeyed the 17th.

Then, in 1923, after seven years of competing at the game's highest levels without winning a national championship, it looked as if Bobby finally had the US Open in his hands. The Championship was played at the Inwood Country Club, near New York City. Jones had begun the last round three strokes ahead of Bobby Cruickshank, four ahead of Jock Hutchison and five in front of Walter Hagen.

One of the early starters, Jones had played the first nine in 39, but 35 in would give him 74, which would be good enough to win, and he had not been over 35 on the second nine in three rounds. Two quick birdies put him in position to finish with 72 if he could par the three closing holes. He would win easily.

Knowing he had been over par on those three holes only once before, Bobby became overconfident and eased up. After a good drive on the 16th, he pushed his second shot out of bounds, and only luck saved a bogey five, when a pulled shot with his second ball bounced off a knoll and rebounded on to the green. He lost another stroke at the 17th and now he needed a par four on the long and difficult 18th to shoot the 74 he wanted.

Losing those two strokes seemed to take something out of him. He played a short drive, then hooked his spoon second close to the tee of the 12th hole, alongside the 18th green. To make his four now, he would have to play a soft pitch over a bunker and have it stop

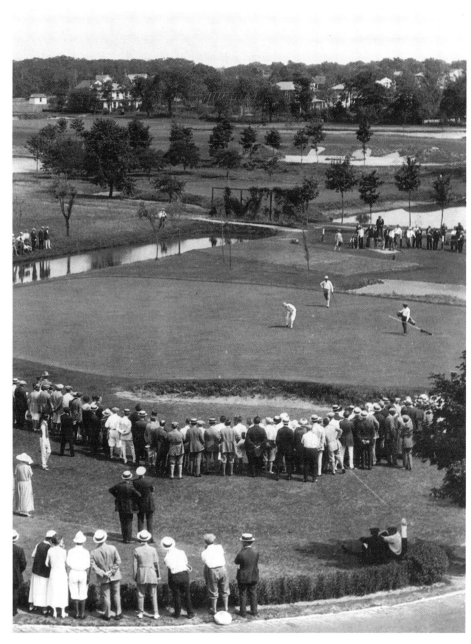

Jones putts on the 18th at Inwood Country Club.

close to the hole. Unnerved, he took too much turf; his ball dropped into the bunker and he made six. Some time later, Bobby Cruickshank birdied the 18th, tying Jones and forcing a play-off the next day.

Over 8,000 fans turned out for the play-off, racing for position as the two men struggled back and forth, first one gaining a stroke, then the other. Only three of the first fifteen holes were halved, and at the end of the 17th they were level. It all came down to the 18th once again, the hole Jones had butch-ered and that Cruickshank had played so well. Cruickshank first. Needing a good, solid drive, he lunged feebly at the ball and moved it barely 150 yards, behind a clump of trees. Jones next. Swinging smoothly, he drove his ball at least 100 yards beyond Cruickshank's, but on to a patch of bare ground off the right edge of the fairway.

With no hope of reaching the green, Cruickshank laid up short of the pond in front, relying on a pitch and a putt to save his four.

Bobby had a clean lie, but his ball lay about 195 yards from the cup; if he didn't hit it cleanly, the ball would probably drop into the water and he would lose. Bobby set himself quickly and tore into the ball. It streaked off on a low line, gradually rose into the dull gray sky, cleared the pond easily, then braked it-

self barely six feet from the cup. Throughout his career Jones would play no more decisive shot than this. It won him his first Open, for Cruickshank was struggling to a six.

Bobby nursed his putt close, then tapped it in for par four, and 76 for the round. Cruickshank finished with 78.

This was the beginning of a career no one has matched. Within the next seven seasons Jones would win three more US Opens, lose two others in play-offs, win three British Opens, five US Amateurs and the British Amateur. No one has ever won so many national championships in such a short time.

R.S.

Bobby Jones returns triumphantly to his native Georgia after winning the 1923 US Open.

BYRON NELSON

1-iron to the 4th at Spring Mill in the 1939 US Open

Byron Nelson hadn't reached his peak when the US Open moved to the Spring Mill Course of the Philadelphia Country Club in 1939. His best years lay ahead, years when he would demolish the competition on the PGA Tour. He had won the Masters Tournament in 1937, but the Masters hadn't yet grown into one of the game's four principal competitions. Only the US PGA Championship and the US Open mattered on the American side of the Atlantic, and the Open counted most. Nelson hadn't won it, but he was only 27 and he had years ahead of him.

Nelson was an innovator. He had an upright swing and moved into the ball with a pronounced lateral shift of his hips, his knees dipping at impact. He had developed a new method of striking the ball that eliminated what had been a chronic hook, became the most reliable driver the game has ever known, and no one ever played better long irons. He was not one of the game's great putters,

Nelson putts in the play-off.

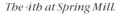

The 4th at Spring Mill.

but a man who consistently plays his approaches within 15 feet of the hole doesn't have to be.

Ralph Guldahl had won the previous two US Opens, but Sam Snead was the heavy favorite at Spring Mill. He had nearly won two years earlier in his first attempt, but Guldahl had shot a record score of 281 to beat him.

A long driver, excellent iron player and superb around the greens, Snead seemed suited to Spring Mill. It measured 6,786 yards, which might not seem impressive, but it had a par of 69, with lots of par four holes in the 450-yards-and-beyond range. Three of its par three holes measured 200 yards and more, and the 18th, its lone par five, stretched 555 yards uphill.

While it might have suited Snead, it was perfect for Nelson. To illustrate, Nelson was off to a shaky start, dropping four strokes to par over the first seven holes, but then he came to the 8th, a par four that stretched 479 yards, beginning from a low tee and playing over the crest of a hill to a plateau, with the green sitting in the distance. Nelson strung one of his perfectly straight drives, then rifled a 2-iron on to the green. He made his four and played the remaining ten holes in one under par, finishing with 72.

Nelson had followed with 73 in the second round, which left him six strokes off the lead, but he picked up two strokes in the third. He began the fourth round with a birdie at the 1st, a strong 450-yard par four, but lost that stroke at the 3rd, then played thirteen consecutive pars. A putt finally fell at the 17th, dropping him to one under par, and he played the 18th in a steady par five for 68. He was in with 284, eight strokes over par. Now he could only wait.

Snead seemed certain to win. He had opened with 68, then followed with 71 and 73, and had gon : into the last round

tied with Craig Wood, Denny Shute, the 1933 British Open Champion, and Clayton Heafner, a gruff redhead from North Carolina, a stroke behind Johnny Bulla.

Both Bulla and Heafner fell apart in the afternoon, but Sam returned to his form of the early rounds. With two holes to play, he had the Championship won. Then he bogeyed the 17th. No harm done; a five on the 18th would bring him in at 283, a score nobody could beat.

Angry because he had played the 17th badly, Snead rushed his shot from the 18th tee, swung quickly and hooked the ball into the rough. Still angry, he hurried a 2-wood, topping the ball and hitting into a bunker. Instead of the five, he made eight and dropped from sight.

Both Wood and Shute came in later with 284s, tying Nelson and setting up the first three-man play-off since Francis Ouimet had beaten Harry Vardon and Ted Ray back in 1913.

Shute played badly in the play-off and dropped out, but Nelson and Wood tied at 68, Nelson holing a putt of eight feet to birdie the 18th after Wood had driven into the crowd and hit a spectator. Craig missed from four feet. Now there would be a second 18-hole play-off.

Nelson hit his stride in the second play-off round. He took a one-stroke lead after birdieing the 3rd, and then stepped on to the tee of the 4th, a 453-yard par four that was among Spring Mill's strongest holes, calling for a long-iron second, Nelson's strength. The tee is set on low ground behind a small pond. Beyond the pond, the ground rises sharply to the crest of a hill and then the fairway swings right and falls away gently to the green.

Nelson rifled his drive over the crest of the hill on to a level patch on the left side of the fairway. After Wood had played his approach, Byron reached for his 1-iron, a club he had taken off the rack as soon as he had signed a contract with a manufacturer a year earlier.

He had a good distance to go, but this was a shot made for him. He set himself, moved into the ball with his usual shift of the hips and nipped the ball perfectly off the turf. The shot never left the flagstick. He played it high and it came to ground immediately in front of the green, hopped on, rolled to the right of the flagstick, curled left and trickled into the hole. An eagle two. The shot demoralized Wood; Byron had opened a three-stroke lead, and the play-off was over.

"It ran into the hole like a rat," Nelson grinned. "It startled me," he admitted. "I bogeyed the next hole, so I said to myself, 'Don't let it bother you.'"

It didn't at all. He lost a few strokes along the way, but he shot 70 and beat Wood by three strokes.

Nelson's 1-iron is on display at the Museum of the USGA in Far Hills, New Jersey. When Byron visited the museum some years ago, the club was taken from the rack and he was persuaded to hit a few balls. After he had hit two or three, he was asked how the old club felt.

"Like a hunk of lead," he said.

R.S.

Byron Nelson with the US Open trophy in 1939 as Ralph Guldahl, the winner in 1937 and 1938, reluctantly releases his hold on the silverware.

LARRY MIZE

pitch and run to the 11th at Augusta in the 1987 US Masters

The picture one has of the 11th hole at the Augusta National Golf Club is of the entrance to a dangerous, though beautiful place. A par four of 445 yards, it begins within a forest, passes through a long, rather narrow corridor on to a rolling hillside, all the while canting from right to left, and falls to a spreading green beside a sinister, gathering pond. To the right, a broad, rippling lawn; to the left, the darkening water.

Mounting the hillside, one is fully exposed to the delicious torments of Augusta's Amen Corner, a sequence of three holes where prayers are never far from the mind. As the 1987 US Masters drew to its climax, the farthest thought from anyone's mind was that Larry Mize would choose this setting to perform a miracle.

Mize is a slender, appealing fellow with a fullish swing, rather less than rhythmic for its pause at the top, but one that proceeds easily, without effort. He is long enough and he's a good iron player, with an assertive touch in the short game. His style is not to show much as he goes along, but there is grit inside. A rising player in 1987, he had not yet crashed through in a big event.

The Masters had been a furious chase. First Curtis Strange had led after two rounds, and well into the third, until he dumped his second shot into the pond at the 15th. Then it was Greg Norman, Roger Maltbie and Ben Crenshaw drawing ahead, with Bernhard Langer close behind. Within range were Seve Ballesteros, T.C. Chen and Mize. Well into the fourth round eight players had closed within a stroke of the lead, and at the end it was down to four.

A rash of birdies by Mize on the inward nine, the same from Norman, and then Ballesteros came back with two of his own, and they were all tied with Crenshaw. But Ben bogeyed the 17th, so it would be sudden death among Norman, Ballesteros and Mize.

Seve was eliminated on the 10th, the first play-off hole, crestfallen after missing a short putt and failing to match the pars by Norman and Mize. Now there were two: Norman, the dominant player in the game in 1986, and Mize, the quiet native of Augusta, who had dreamed of playing in the Masters one day.

They moved to the 11th, Augusta National's most difficult hole. Both men drove well. Mize, 194 yards from the hole, played first. Using a 5-iron, he pushed the shot on to the lawn beside the green, far away from the hole. From 164 yards, Norman also played to the right, but he reached the fringe of the green with his 7-iron. Earlier in the day Mize had played safely on to the same lawn and had saved his par, but on that occasion he had been 10 yards closer.

Larry Mize, chipping to the 11th hole in the play-off.

Mize chips at the 11th, as Norman watches...

... holes out, and leaps for joy.

Now he was 46 yards from the hole and he knew the next shot would run quickly on the slick green, which fed everything toward the dreaded pond.

Mize took time to collect himself, then chose his sand iron. He seemed calm as he took his position over the ball, glancing toward the flagstick and the water beyond. The shot flew low, bounced twice before it reached the green, then scurried across the glassy surface, drawn ever closer to the hole. Before anyone realized it would be very close indeed, quite suddenly it was in. Mize covered his face in disbelief, then leaped and danced on to the green, past the immobile figure of Norman. Greg stood transfixed; it was the second time in less than a year that an upstart had holed out from an impossible position to snatch a major tournament from him. There would be no searching response;

Mize's shot had struck at his vitals. Norman could still halve the hole, but his putt was never high enough to have a chance.

One could sympathize with Norman's disappointment, but it was one of those occasions when Mize was always going to be the winner. He had driven longer and with greater effect on the 10th than either Norman or Ballesteros, and he had played a better approach than either man. He was cooler and less inclined to force himself. Watching the drama, one shuddered to think what must have gone through Norman's mind as he saw the ball disappear. But there was much to like in the picture of the young man reaching into the most fearful part of the course with this graceful little running shot, and ending things with such a thump.

C.B.

ARNOLD PALMER

driver to the 1st at Cherry Hills in the 1960 US Open

A frame-by-frame record of Arnold Palmer's amazing 346-yard drive to the 1st green on his way to victory in the final round at Cherry Hills.

The most attractive player in the game in 1960, Arnold Palmer always drew a crowd.

Arnold Palmer ruled golf in 1960. He was the greatest hero since Bobby Jones, more popular than the clinically cold Ben Hogan or the warm and pleasant Byron Nelson, or even the colorful Sam Snead had been. Palmer was the swashbuckling adventurer who played the game with courage and élan, never backing down from the daring shot, always shooting for the flag.

Without question, he was the most at-tractive figure in the game, the player who would draw the galleries. If Palmer was in a tournament, spectators would turn out to watch. If he wasn't they wouldn't. His fanatically loyal gallery looked on everyone else as an enemy, a pretender to Arnold's kingdom.

Like Hogan before him, Palmer attacked a course. He threw himself into every shot, and while he wasn't the longest driver in the game, he looked it, and he was indeed the most accurate. He was an exceptional iron player and he chipped like a magician, but he was weak with the wedge, and while he holed his share of long putts, he was not an exceptional putter.

Palmer played for the sheer joy of it, and he was possibly the most confident golfer who ever lived. He came on to the tour late in 1954, shortly after winning the US Amateur, convinced he could beat Hogan any time Ben wanted to play.

By 1960 Palmer had reason to believe he might have beaten Hogan in his prime. He had won the Masters twice, his second earlier in 1960 by birdieing the last two holes at Augusta and beating Ken Venturi by a single stroke. While he hadn't won a US Open, he had played steadily since 1953 and had been in position to win twice, placing

seventh in 1957, six strokes behind Cary Middlecoff, and fifth in 1959. Needing a round under 70, he shot 74, and finished four strokes behind Billy Casper.

He had been on a hot streak in the weeks leading up to the 1960 US Open. In addition to the Masters, he had won four other Tournaments, lost another in a play-off, and had placed among the first five in eleven of his eighteen starts. Clearly he was the popular choice, but he had fallen seven strokes behind Mike Souchak after three rounds and, more important, trailed fourteen men. Souchak had a score of 208, Palmer 215.

Palmer sat at lunch eating a cheeseburger, drinking iced tea and talking with Ken Venturi, Bob Rosburg and Bob Drum, a reporter with a Pittsburgh newspaper. The conversation was dull until Palmer brought it to life. "I may shoot 65," he said. "What would that do?" "Nothing," Drum snarled. "You're too far back." Palmer's eyes blazed. "The hell I am," he snapped. "A 65 would give me 280, and 280 wins Opens." He pushed back his chair and stormed from the room.

The Championship was being played at the Cherry Hills Country Club, in a suburb of Denver, Colorado, about 5,000 feet about sea level. While it mea-

sured 7,004 yards, it played much shorter, because golf balls fly much farther at that altitude.

Cherry Hills began with a short parfour hole of 346 yards with a creek flowing along the left and a belt of rough blocking the entrance to the green. A good, strong drive could reach the green, but Palmer had tried in every round and failed each time. Still, you can't be conservative when you're seven strokes behind.

Arnold went for it again. Throwing every ounce of himself into the shot, he drilled the ball straight at the target. It hung in the sky for what seemed like minutes, came down heading straight for the flagstick, bounded through the rough, and rolled on to the green, pulling up 25 feet from the cup.

Arnold's gallery roared, then dashed down the hill toward the green; Palmer was off on one of the game's legendary rounds. His putt for an eagle two slipped past the hole, but he made his birdie, played the first nine in 30, came home in 35, shooting the 65 he said he might, and his 280 beat Jack Nicklaus by two strokes.

The entire round was sparked by that first drive, a telling stroke that set up one of the game's most stirring finishes.

R.S.

LEW WORSHAM

wedge to the 18th at Tam O'Shanter in the 1953 World Championship

The World Championship of Golf was never one of the game's great events, even though it offered more prize money than anyone dreamed of in the late 1940s and early 1950s. The winner would receive $25,000 as first prize, then play a series of exhibition matches worth another $25,000.

The Tournament was played at the Tam O'Shanter Country Club in the suburbs of Chicago, and run by George S. May, a Barnum-like former Bible salesman who turned golf tournaments into carnivals, insisting, for example, players wear numbers on their backs, like sprinters, so the gallery could identify them (attaching players' names to the backs of their caddies came later). The players put up with it because it paid well.

The World Championship came along at a time when televised golf was only beginning in the United States and most tournaments were shown only locally. The US Open went on the network for the first time in 1954, but the World Championship was given network coverage in 1953, the first American golf tournament broadcast from coast to coast.

Lew Worsham in 1947, the year he won the US Open.

Golf was becoming wildly popular by then. Ben Hogan had become a national hero by winning the Masters, the US Open and the British Open earlier in the year, and President Dwight D. Eisenhower was serving his first term, occasionally slipping away from the White House for a round at the Augusta National Golf Club.

May owned the Tam O'Shanter Club, so he could do with it what he wanted. He built a permanent grandstand behind the 18th green, again the first ever – or the first anyone knew of – and he lowered the admission charge to only $1. Thousands of people came, possibly more to wander around a lush setting on a sultry August afternoon than to watch the golfers.

Julius Boros had won the 1952 World, but he complained that the exhibitions had taken him away from tournament golf so often that he had lost his competitive edge. Nevertheless, he opened with 68, then shot 71 and 72 in the next two rounds. He might have been right; he closed with 74, not nearly good enough.

Lew Worsham had won the 1947 US Open, beating Sam Snead in a play-off at the St Louis Country Club, another of Snead's haunting failures. By coincidence, that was the first golf tournament ever telecast. A local station had mounted a camera in a flatbed truck and parked it close by the 18th green. The camera showed only one hole, but not much had changed over the last six years; the national audience would see only the 18th at the Tam.

A delighted Lew Worsham eyes a pile of newspaper clippings trumpeting his winning eagle 2.

Tam's 18th was a 410-yard par four that curved gently right. The green's entrance was wide open and a small brook crossed the fairway yards short. Worsham rifled a long and straight drive into prime position, no more than 110 yards from the green.

Worsham knew exactly the club he wanted. He had played the hole seven times by them – in the All-America, a tournament that preceded the World over the same course a week earlier – and had used his wedge in six of them. He'd go with it again. At first the shot didn't seem to come off the club as Worsham had planned. He had to pitch close enough to the hole for a reasonable chance for a birdie, but this ball wouldn't even reach the green.

It did indeed come to earth a yard or so short, but then it hopped on, began rolling toward the hole, kept rolling on and on, and then, with Harper watching, it tumbled into the cup for an eagle 2. Worsham had nipped Harper by a stroke, finished the round in 68 and won the World Championship with a 72-hole score of 278.

Unorthodox though it might have been, the shot was effective. It was also sensational, and it had positive consequences. Millions had seen it on television, which helped boost the game's popularity in the United States.

It had positive effects for Worsham as well. In addition to the $25,000 first prize, he picked up an additional $40,000 in exhibitions the following year. Years later he had the club mounted on the wall of his house. Looking at it, he said, "Someone once suggested I have a plaque hung beside it saying, 'This wedge built this house.'"

The shot was voted the sports thrill of the year in a newspaper poll, and years later Worsham was still asked how it felt.

" 'Good, man,' I tell them. 'Good.' "

R.S.

While Boros had shot 68 in the first round, Worsham had beaten him by three strokes, shooting 65, but he hadn't kept up that level of scoring; 72 in the second round and 73 in the third had dropped him out of the lead, but he was playing better in the fourth round, closing in on Chandler Harper, a fellow Virginian, who had won the 1950 US PGA Championship.

Worsham was in the last group of three players, and Harper was just in front of him. Worsham dropped a stroke on the 16th. Now he knew he would have to birdie the last two holes to win. He made his birdie on the 17th, holing a putt of eight feet, but then word drifted back that Harper had birdied the 18th, dropping a lovely pitch within a foot of the cup. Now Worsham would have to match it to tie.

JERRY PATE

*A study in determination,
Jerry Pate follows through
on his picture swing.*

Jerry Pate had come into professional golf with a picture swing, a long, fluid motion played to a lazy tempo that masked the immense power he put into his shots. Because of his swing, he was the envy of many an aspiring tour player, and those who watched him knew he would become a winner one day. Whether it would come to him in his early 20s was another matter, but Pate could hope.

"I'd like to win a US Open to go along with my Amateur. That would give me two majors in my early 20s, like Jack Nicklaus."

Nicklaus had indeed won them both

Are you sure I have two putts to win?

by that age, the Amateur for the first time when he was 19, the Open when he had reached 22. Pate had won the Amateur in 1974, a few weeks before he turned 21. His birthday fell in September; to match Jack's record, he would have to win the 1976 Open.

Until then the US Open hadn't been played in the quadrant of the country east of the Mississippi and south of the Potomac, but shortly before he died, Bobby Jones had written to the US Golf Association (USGA) asking for it to be brought to the Atlanta Athletic Club, his first club. He had grown up playing the East Lake Course, but by the 1970s the Atlanta AC had sold the old property and moved to new quarters in the suburb of Duluth. It was a marvellous facility, with a modern clubhouse and a gymnasium augmented by handball courts and weight-lifting and exercise rooms. It had 27 holes of golf, one nine designed by Joe Finger, and eighteen by Robert Trent Jones.

It wasn't the US Open's greatest course by any means, but it was laid out over a large tract of ground and it had room for more spectators that the USGA normally allows. While ticket sales had been limited to 14,000 for the 1971 Championship at the Merion Golf Club, near Philadelphia, the Atlanta AC was permitted to sell 30,000.

Pate remained an amateur through most of 1975, playing on the Walker Cup Team in the spring and in the US Open, and had joined the tour late in 1975. He played steadily, week after week. By the time the field gathered in Atlanta he had played in 20 of 23 tour tournaments. He was the youngest player on the tour, but even so, it had been quite a strain on him; his weight had dropped from 170 to 160 pounds.

Pate came into the Championship brimming with confidence. He had written to Conrad Rehling, his coach at the University of Alabama, and told him he believed he could win.

Just as he had the year before, John Mahaffey was back in contention, leading after three rounds, with a score of 207. Surprising most of the gallery, Pate had hung around the lead through 54 holes and now trailed Mahaffey by two strokes, but Al Geiberger and Tom Weiskopf looked the more serious threats, Geiberger with 210, and Weiskopf with 211.

Geiberger and Weiskopf completed their 72 holes the next day at 279 and hung around the scorer's tent waiting for Mahaffey and Pate, playing just behind them. Mahaffey had clung to his lead through 14 holes, but Pate caught him with a birdie at the 15th, a par three of more than 200 yards.

Within the next two holes Mahaffey dropped out of the lead. One of the tour's shortest hitters, he hooked his drive into a fairway bunker on the 16th and then three-putted the 17th, falling two strokes behind Pate coming to the 18th, a long and dangerous par four of 460 yards with a pond guarding the front of the green.

Mahaffey drove into the rough and, trying to reach the green with a 3-wood, dropped his second into the pond. His challenge was over.

Pate wasn't safe, though. He needed a four to shoot 278 and beat Geiberger and Weiskopf, but, like Mahaffey, he had driven into the deep bermudagrass rough, a wiry strain that can wrench a club from a man's hands. He might have to lay up with his second and hope for a pitch-and-putt par.

When he arrived at his ball, Pate saw he had been lucky. Instead of snuggling down into the grass, his ball was sitting up, perched in a shaky position atop a few strands. He could play almost any club he wanted. Looking it over, Jerry saw he stood about 190 yards from the hole. He would play a 5-iron. He took out the club, then leaned down to check

🏌 *His birthday fell in September; to match Jack's record, he would have to win the 1976 Open.* 🏌

Pate swings with his smooth action and watches the ball soar.

the ground around the ball. Meantime, the referee, Harry Easterly, the USGA's president, had grown concerned. The ball was not in a very stable position; if it moved, Pate could be penalized. He moved into positon to watch more closely because it would be up to him to call an infraction.

With Easterly hovering close by, Pate grounded his club behind the ball and prepared to play the most important shot of his still infant career. The hole was set in the lower left portion of the kidney-shaped green, on a peninsula jutting into the pond. Two bunkers stood just behind, in a direct line with Pate's shot. None of this seemed to concern Pate. He swung into the ball with as smooth a stroke as you could imagine, looking as if he was hitting nothing more than a practice shot.

The ball covered the flag all the way. It soared high and came down light as a feather, hitting about four feet from the pin and stopping within two feet. As the ball stopped rolling, Mahaffey walked over to Pate and said, "Nice shot."

It was a nice shot indeed; it must rank among the finest ever played in the heat of a competition of this stature, with the Championship at stake and for the first victory of a young man's career. It was a nerveless shot, showing supreme confidence in his swing. Now he had the Open in his hand.

But Jerry wanted to be sure. Before putting, he approached Easterly. "Are you sure I have two putts to win?" he asked. Assured this was indeed the case, Pate holed for the birdie three, raised his right arm, saluting the cheering crowd, then picked his ball from the cup and flung it into the gallery. He had played the final round in 68, and shot 277 for 72 holes, two strokes better than Weiskopf and Geiberger. Like Nicklaus, he had won a US Open at 22.

R.S.

KEN VENTURI

1-iron to the 16th at Congressional in the 1964 US Open

Byron Nelson was considered the finest iron player of his day, an era that included Hogan, Snead, Demaret and others who might otherwise have claimed that honor. Long after his playing days ended, Nelson had been asked one of those silly questions that golf writers and television announcers can never find the will to resist.

"Who, besides yourself, was the greatest iron player you have seen?" Without hesitating Nelson replied, "Ken Venturi — and that includes me."

Whether or not Nelson was being modest, as he always is, he was nevertheless acknowledging a commonly held view that Venturi was, for a time, in a class by himself. He was one of those men who come along every so often with the technical mastery and the instinct that could lift his game on to another level. Many did it with the driver and the putter, others by scrambling, some by the sheer force of will, but in his generation, no one played the full range of irons, from the wedge through the 1-iron, with such brilliance and effect.

Everyone who cares about these things knows the story of the 1964 US Open: how after years of decline Venturi scored one of the most melodramatic and emotional victories in Open history, prevailing over heat prostration, exhaustion, dehydration and the loathsome, insidious doubts that beset the mind when one is struggling back.

The Championship was played at Congressional Country Club, on the outskirts of Washington DC, during a particularly sullen heat wave. This was to be the last year the final two rounds would be staged on Saturday, a gruelling 36-hole finish that tradition had ordained most likely to produce a worthy Champion.

From somewhere deep within him, Venturi was summoning a performance

Neat and compact, Ken Venturi's swing was the envy of his peers.

of astonishing consistency and skill. Time and again his iron shots kept him in the game. Hole after hole he played shots that left him gasping for breath and the gallery gasping in wonder. The stroke that clinched it, Venturi believes, came at the 16th hole of the final round.

This is a long par three of about 215 yards with a green all but surrounded by bunkers. The flagstick that day was set toward the back. Venturi knew he was leading, because he had looked over to the scoreboard and had seen that his was the only score in red figures, but he could not tell by how many strokes.

"All I knew was that if I could par this hole, I would clinch it," Venturi said.

He chose to play a 1-iron. As he prepared himself for the shot he remembered something Nelson had told him: it is easier to aim at the flag than at the green. This advice often helped to focus and concentrate the stroke.

When he was playing well, Venturi recalls, he felt "there was no way they could hide the flag from me," and he was as confident with the 1-iron as he was with any club in his bag.

His club flashed in the muggy air, the ball streaked from the face with a purring whoosh, and never left the flag. It landed on the front of the green, bounced and rolled, and struck the flagstick. It was a majestic stroke. For just an instant the sweltering gallery experienced a chill. It was one of those chilling moments of recognition at witnessing a great occasion, and feeling admiration for the man responsible.

C.B.

Relief at the final green.

Preceding page, the moment of triumph at last for an exhausted Venturi.

TOM WATSON

chip on the 17th at Pebble Beach in the 1982 US Open

❝ *Sometimes, I would fantasize about playing the last four holes for the US Open against Jack Nicklaus.* ❞

By 1982 Tom Watson had established himself as one of the game's best players, but even though he had won the Masters twice and the British Open three times, he had not lifted himself quite on to that level of greatness his talent promised and that he so clearly sought. He had not won the US Open. He might have won at Winged Foot in 1974, and at Medinah in 1975, and he had threatened briefly at Baltusrol in 1980, but he could not seem to find the winning stroke when it mattered most.

Watson was sometimes an erratic driver, although a long one, whose swing seemed to be bound to a single, instinctive rhythm buried deep within him. If there was any criticism of his method, it was that his swing had only one pace, and a rather brisk one it was, so that when the timing was off by just a fraction, his long game suffered.

He was arguably the best putter in the game, deadlier even than Crenshaw, and something of a genius with the short game. His imagination and touch with those nasty little pitches around the green was wonderful to watch. He was one of those players who gave you the impression he might hole anything, and he played these shots fearlessly.

Watson approached the 1982 US Open with mixed feelings. He felt that his long game was not in top form, but the Championship was being played at Pebble Beach, a course that had shaped his game and one that he loved.

"While I was attending college at Stanford, I used to come out early and play alone. Sometimes, I would fantasize about playing the last four holes for the US Open against Jack Nicklaus," Watson remembers.

It must have occurred to him, too, that Nicklaus had won five tournaments at Pebble Beach – three Bing Crosby Pro-Ams, the 1961 US Amateur Championship and the 1972 US Open.

Nicklaus was by no means finished with his plunder of the major events; he was on the prowl for his fifth US Open.

The weather had been cold, dank and misty throughout the week. After two rounds, Nicklaus and Watson were tied at even par, five strokes behind Bruce Devlin, the surprise leader. Devlin was then 44 and played tournament golf only part-time.

Watson shot 68 in the third round and Bill Rogers 69. They shared the lead at 212. Nicklaus, after a 71, was three strokes behind.

After a shaky start on Sunday, another chilly day, Nicklaus shook up the field by reeling off five consecutive birdies and climbing into a tie for the lead. The battle had been fairly joined. At one point five men were within a stroke of one another. Then, one by one, they began missing strokes. Nicklaus bogied the 8th, Watson missed a tiddler at the short 7th, Rogers bogeyed the 10th and began to fall away. Watson had holed two long putts at the 10th and 14th to stay even with Nicklaus, and the Championship was now between them.

When Nicklaus finished at 284, four under, Watson was just stepping on to the tee at the long, par three 17th hole. The markers had been set at 209 yards, the flagstick on the left side, toward the rear of the wide, hourglass-shaped green.

Watson chose a 2-iron and pulled the shot into the thick, clumpy kikuyu rough beside the green. A grimace of disappointment now and a murmur from the gallery, because the flagstick was perhaps 12 feet from the edge of the green. Not much room there, and Watson's ball was 20 feet from the hole, with a foot of left-to-right break. He would have to play the next stroke downhill, across a green that was mercilessly slick. The odds on stopping the ball anywhere near the hole could hardly have been less favorable, and a

From ankle-deep rough on the edge of the 17th green at Pebble Beach, Tom Watson plays the decisive shot of the 1982 US Open and dances in delight as the ball curls into the hole.

❛ *I've been dreaming about this moment since I was 10 years old.* ❜

bogey would surely cost him the Open.

As Watson settled himself for the shot, his shoes and clubhead vanished from sight, swallowed by the heavy grass. Using a sand wedge, he played a brisk, slicing stroke and lobbed the ball just on to the green. It hopped twice and curled smartly into the hole. An astonishing stroke.

Watson danced across the green and pointed at his caddie, Bruce Edwards.

"When I saw the ball lying well in the grass," Tom said later, "I told him the shot was makeable, and I meant to hole it."

At the long 18th Watson pitched a 9-iron to within 15 feet, then holed the putt for another birdie, a final round of 70 and a total of 282, two strokes better than Nicklaus. The final flourish was unnecessary, but sweet.

"I've been dreaming about this moment since I was 10 years old," Watson exclaimed. "It is the Championship I most wanted to win, on one of my favourite golf courses. All week I drove so badly I wondered how I could play some of the holes. Somehow, I gutted it out at the end of each round. I couldn't have written the script better."

Weeks later Watson and a group of friends strolled to the 17th green and tried to duplicate the shot. There were six or seven players, including the cartoonist Hank Ketcham, the golf course architect Robert Trent Jones Jr and Frank Tatum, a former USGA president. Each man tried two or three shots. No one came close.

C.B.

FRANCIS OUIMET

approach to the 17th at The Country Club, Brookline, in the 1913 US Open

OUIMET WORLD'S GOLF CHAMPION

Twenty-Year-Old Amateur Defeats Famous British Professionals for Open Title.

REMARKABLE GOLF FEAT

Covers the 18-Hole Course at Brookline in 72 Strokes— Vardon 77, Ray 78.

SPLENDID DISPLAY OF NERVE

First Amateur to Win American Open Championship—Big Gallery Makes Demonstration at Finish.

America acclaimed the dramatic victory of Francis Ouimet in the 1913 US Open over Harry Vardon and Ted Ray, for it brought an end to British domination of the game.

Francis Ouimet was 20 years old in 1913. He had grown up playing golf on a rude course he and his older brother Wilfred had laid out behind their house in Brookline, Massachusetts, a suburb of Boston. He had played high school golf with some success, taken a job with a sporting goods manufacturer after graduation and earlier in the year had won the State Amateur Championship.

Taking some vacation time, he had entered the National Amateur and had played a very strong match against the great Jerry Travers in early September, losing on the 34th hole by 3 and 2.

Trying to assemble a strong amateur field for the Open, Robert Watson, the president of the United States Golf Association (USGA), had persuaded Francis to enter, but Ouimet had used all his vacation time for the Amateur, wouldn't ask for more and didn't intend to play. Seeing his name among the entrants, however, John Merrill, his supervisor at the Wright and Ditson retail store, suggested that since Francis had entered, he should play. Thus Merrill turned the 1913 Championship into the most significant US Open ever played.

The stylish Harry Vardon, one of the greatest golfers who has ever played the game, was touring the country with Ted Ray, the 1912 British Open Champion, the longest hitter of his time. They were expected to decide the Championship between them and, indeed, they were tied after 72 holes, with 304, the best totals after a dreary, rainy day.

One by one the American hopefuls had fallen, and of the few men still on the course, only Ouimet stood within range, but with very slim prospects. Needing 78 to win, or 79 to tie, he had gone out in 43, then threw away two more strokes by scoring five on the 10th, a little par three of 140 yards. Now he would have to play the last eight holes in one under par to tie. A five on

Left, Francis Ouimet photographed in 1913 and, above, an illustration of the decisive approach to the 17th, with Vardon, Ray and Ouimet's 10-year-old caddie watching.

the 12th, where he had counted on a four, hurt – now he would have to play the last six holes in two under. He chipped in for a birdie three at the 13th, then saved himself once again by holing a testing putt of nine feet to hold par on the 16th, a par three.

Now he would have to birdie one of the last two holes to match the Englishmen's scores. The 17th was a 360-yards par four that doglegged left around a bunker. Taking no chances, Francis drove well to the right, then surveyed his approach. He would have to make his birdie here, because the 18th was much too strong a hole, playing 410 yards to a green raised above the level of

the fairway.

After a momentary pause, Ouimet drew out a jigger, a versatile instrument that originated as a trouble club designed to help the golfer escape from tangled rough, cart tracks, dirt roads and unraked bunkers. It had a longish shaft, a shallow head and the approximate loft of a modern 4-iron.

Setting himself firmly on the soft ground, Ouimet swung into the ball. He made solid contact and watched as it rose into the dark sky, flying straight at the flagstick. He could see it was a terrific shot, just what he wanted to give him his chance at the birdie he needed so badly. The ball slowly began its

Ouimet lines up a putt.

descent, then plunged on to the soft green and braked about 15 feet beyond the hole.

Standing nearby, Travers whispered to a friend, "Won't we hear a yell if he holes it?"

Telling himself to be sure to give the putt a chance, Ouimet struck the ball firmly; it rolled down the inclining green, slammed into the back of the cup, then dropped in for the three. A par at the 18th and Ouimet had tied Vardon and Ray, setting up a play-off the next day.

Francis played much the better golf the next day and reached the 17th leading Vardon by one stroke and Ray by five. Trying to save distance and make up the stroke he needed by cutting the dog-leg, Vardon drove into the bunker and made five. Francis played the hole exactly as he had in the fourth round – a safe drive to the fairway, another jigger to 15 feet and another putt that fell. Three strokes ahead now, he couldn't lose. He finished with 72, Vardon shot 75 and Ray, 78.

Because it showed that American golfers had developed so well they could beat the best of the British, the 1913 US Open is remembered as the most significant ever played, and the putt Francis Ouimet holed on the 17th, earning him the tie, among the most significant in American golf.

R.S.

JERRY BARBER

Be warned. What you are about to read might easily spring from the imagination of Robin Williams. It is what would happen if Baron Münchhausen had been allowed on the professional tour. It concerns Jerry Barber, a noted cut-purse who picked the pockets of many unsuspecting pros, and Don January, the unwilling victim.

Barber had everything against him. He had poor vision and carried different spectacles for different times of the day. He stood barely 5ft 5in. tall and he couldn't hit the ball far. His action could not be described as a swing; rather, it

looked to have been assembled from a dozen separate parts, none of which fitted. His only chance was to become a world-class putter and chipper. This he did rather well.

Others began to notice that no matter where Barber hit the ball, he was always putting and chipping for pars and birdies. Unlike the others, though, he was making them. He became Sam Snead's favorite partner in money matches. Snead called him Rock. Neither man, it will be recalled, was known for his willingness to part with money, and as a team they rarely did so.

Barber was capable of holing anything with that putter, a nondescript and distasteful implement with a singu-

lar deformity at the bottom that bore a vague resemblance to brass. In Barber's hands, this lifeless lump was transformed. Don't imagine that any players of later times – Ben Crenshaw, Seve Ballesteros, Gary Koch, Mark Calcavecchia – are to be reckoned great putters while Barber lives. And his chipping and pitching were not far behind.

Barber was 45 years old when the field gathered for the 1961 US PGA Championship at Olympia Fields, a stern test on the south side of Chicago. Arnold Palmer, Jack Nicklaus and Gary Player were dividing up the major titles then, although Gene Littler had won the US Open that year and fellows like Julius Boros and Billy Casper were in their prime. But the man playing best of all that week was Don January, a slim Texan with a slow gait, a slashing swing and the disposition of a gunfighter. Off the course January was an amiable fellow with a dry but wicked sense of humor and popular with his fellows. On it, he was a hard customer.

The pairings for the final round sent January out with fellow-Texan Ernie Vossler and the tenacious Barber, who frequently looked as if he were playing in a different group. Barber drove into a tree on the third hole, hit it out left-handed, knocked a 4-wood 40 yards short of the green and pitched into the hole. Mark down a par four.

He topped his drive at the 10th, hit two more shots and then chipped in from heavy grass. Another par.

January meanwhile was playing glorious shots, long and accurate, and had built a lead of five strokes. Reaching the 11th, a par three, he played a majestic stroke that flew straight at the hole, hit the flagstick and ricocheted into a bunker. Playing next, Barber pulled his ball into a tree and hit a branch; the ball bounced out and on to the green two and a half feet from the hole. A birdie, and a stroke gained.

Jerry Barber in a reflective moment.

❝ *I was not thinking of anything but holing that putt. When I hit it, I thought, holy smoke, it's got a chance.* ❞

January was no stranger to spectacular shots. He had holed from a bunker on the final green to win the 1956 Texas Centennial Open in Dallas, his first on the Tour, but this was too much.

"I was playing like hell, good enough to beat all those guys," January recalled, taking no pleasure in the retelling. The words came from the corner of his mouth, teeth clenched: "I'm four or five shots ahead of him all day long and he

Jerry Barber, on the right, stares straight ahead as he sinks the 60-foot putt, while Don January (left foreground) and Ernie Vossler (center foreground) look on amazed.

Opposite, the 1988 British Open saw Seve Ballesteros turn the tide against Nicky Price and Nick Faldo.

keeps pulling stuff like that." It would get worse.

January finally made a bogey at the 16th while Barber serenely holed a putt of 25 feet for a birdie. Two strokes separated them.

It was nearly eight o'clock now, and Barber changed from dark glasses to light ones before hitting his next tee shot. His driver bounced nearly a foot behind the tee peg and his ball ducked into the rough about 130 yards ahead. Another mediocre stroke down the fairway, and then a 9-iron, pulled badly, 40 feet from the hole. January hit three gorgeous shots — a drive, a 3-iron that covered the flag but went just too far and a magnificent chip that nearly fell in.

"I don't know how Don's ball stayed out," Barber said sweetly. Just as sweetly, Jerry's long putt, with six inches of left-to-right break, dropped in. So it was on to the 18th, a par four of 436 yards, with Barber still two strokes behind.

January hooked his drive into a fairway bunker and took two more shots to reach the big green. Barber drove well, but he pulled his 3-iron approach to the far left side. Another huge putt followed, this one nearly 60 feet across a ledge that ran diagonally between his ball and the hole.

Barber had the habit of practicing long putts. "That's how you develop a good putting stroke and a feel for distance, not by practicing 10 and 15 footers," he said. Confidence, too. "I was not thinking of anything but holing that putt. When I hit it, I thought, holy smoke, it's got a chance."

The ball rolled on, climbed on to the ledge and then swerved right, hunting the hole. Leaning on their putters, January and Vossler watched as it rolled on and on. And in.

A thunderous cheer exploded from the gallery. January was too stunned to move.

"I had him by two shots and figured a five would beat him. I couldn't believe it," he said. He could still win if he holed his 14-foot uphill putt, but he was mortally wounded now. "There wasn't a prayer of making mine, and I didn't," he said ruefully. "In the play-off I shot 68 and the little so-and-so beat me by a stroke."

Barber had made up four strokes in three holes with putts of roughly 20, 40 and 60 feet, none more improbable than the last. Fabulous would not be too strong a word to use for putting of this order. Maybe it was common in Willie Park's day, but nothing like it had been seen in this century, certainly not in a major championship.

C.B.

TURNING THE TIDE

LEE TREVINO

chip on the 17th at Muirfield in the 1972 British Open

By July 1972 Jack Nicklaus had won both the Masters Tournament and the US Open, and he was in hot pursuit of that will-o'-the-wisp, the professional Grand Slam, needing only the British Open and the US PGA, the final two legs.

The British Open was played at Muirfield, which might be the best golf course in the British Isles. While it is more like a meadowland course than a true links, it is influenced by the sea winds that rip in from the Firth of Forth, just over a rise bordering the 5th hole.

Only one factor was missing: the wind was calm.

Nicklaus had led every round of the Masters and the US Open, but he had fallen behind after 18 holes at Muirfield and had gone into the fourth round trailing Lee Trevino by six strokes. Realizing he had to shoot something like 64 to win, he went about trying.

It was never wise to underestimate Nicklaus. Although winning seemed hopeless, he began making birdies and before long he had actually moved into the lead.

The 17th at Muirfield, site of Trevino's dramatic chip on the last day.

The ground is firm and fast, and a rolling ball often does peculiar things bouncing over its humps and hollows. Muirfield's bunkers are deep and steeply walled; one doesn't escape with a medium iron, one blasts out and gives up a stroke rather than risk losing more. Until irrigation systems changed the nature of links golf, one didn't fly approach shots to Muirfield's greens and expect them to hold; they wouldn't, because the ground was simply too firm.

Doug Sanders described how the game must be played under those conditions. "You skip it, hop it, bump it, run it, hit under it and on top of it, and hope for the right bounce."

Above and opposite, Lee Trevino runs through some of his repertoire of inventive shots and demonstrative gestures.

Trevino, meanwhile, had been playing some amazing golf himself. Over the first three rounds he had chipped in twice and holed out from a bunker on the way to shooting a solid 71–70–66. This put him into the last round at 207, a stroke ahead of Tony Jacklin.

Nicklaus was playing ahead of Trevino and Jacklin, and had drawn even with them as he approached the 16th hole, a good par three of 188 yards, needing one more birdie for the 64. He

wasn't to make it. Jack bogeyed there, falling a stroke behind, and then failed to birdie the 17th, a par five. Now the third leg of the Grand Slam hinged on what Trevino and Jacklin might do on those last few holes.

Both men made their figures on the 16th, but then Trevino made an error on the 17th. He stepped away from his ball twice when first a photographer and then his assistant broke through the ropes and ran from one side of the fairway to the other. Evidently they upset Lee's composure; normally the most

❧ Hey, this isn't over yet. ❧

Once again Lee Trevino takes hold of the Open trophy.

reliable driver in the game, he pulled his ball into a fairway bunker and had no hope of reaching the green in the regulation three strokes. He had to play safely out, then pulled his third into the rough short of the green.

Jacklin, meantime, was playing the

hole perfectly: a solid drive to the fairway, a good second that left him a little pitch to the green, about 15 feet short of the hole. Trevino's ball came out of the rough with no spin on it and raced across the green into the fringe rough. He would surely fall one stroke behind Jacklin here, possibly two.

Trevino had played to the green before Jacklin and had walked ahead feeling rather disgusted with himself. He faced a troubling shot. The green was extremely fast and Trevino's ball would have to fight the grain all the way to the hole. He took hardly any time sizing it up and chipped before Jacklin had reached his ball to mark it. It was as if he didn't care.

The ball hopped over the collar and on to the green, ran true to the hole, then dived into the cup. He had saved his par five and had holed his third chip shot of the week.

Jacklin was shaken so badly he rolled his first putt three feet past the cup. Watching from the grassy bank, Lee said to himself, "Hey, this isn't over yet."

It was, though. Jacklin missed coming back, and Trevino moved a stroke ahead, with only the punishing 18th to play. While it measured 447 yards, Muirfield's home hole was playing as short as it ever had. To be sure he could drive without delay, Trevino took his time walking to the tee, then drove well down the fairway, avoiding the bunkers staggered on either side. After Jacklin's drive caught the rough and he bunkered his second shot, Trevino lofted an 8-iron a few feet past the hole. His two putts for the par were a formality.

Trevino admitted later he wasn't trying very hard when he chipped in on the 17th. He felt the photographers had cost him the Championship, but as the ball had fallen into the hole, he thought of Jacklin and said to himself, "That may have been the straw that broke the camel's back."   R.S.

LANNY WADKINS

*wedge approach to the 18th at the PGA National
in the 1983 Ryder Cup*

If Lanny Wadkins is not the fastest player in the game, the other fellow's name is not generally known. Gene Sarazen, a noted speed merchant, used to say, "Miss 'em quick." Wadkins would say, "Make 'em now." He goes after things with an impetuous flourish, not reckless, mind you, but not exactly meticulous either.

To Wadkins, golf is a stick and a ball and a powerful flail. He's a throwback to the days when burly Scots heaved their hickory shafts at the ball as hard as they could, and if Providence would not take

clearly than it can be seen.

"He has no reverse in his engine, only forward gears," said Don January, a Dallas neighbour and, like Wadkins, a former US PGA Champion. "Lanny doesn't look too good playing sometimes, but you can forget grips and backswings and all that; just listen to the crack. He flat nails it in the backside. And you can't hide the pin from him, 'cause he'll find it and go get it."

Wadkins tends to play in streaks, and when money is on the line, his fellow pros say no one is more likely to come

The 18th at PGA National.

it in hand, then the Devil could take it.

Wadkins pays little attention to criticism of his style, which is somewhat unorthodox. He isn't too particular about how he holds the club, the narrow stance is entirely his own and his swing is a blur that can be heard rather more

through with a telling stroke. He can be a terror in matches, where his bold, impulsive play can shake the most formidable opponent.

Not surprisingly, the Ryder Cup seems to bring out the best in him. He has been a mainstay of five American

Above and opposite, aggression oozes from Lanny Wadkins on the golf course.

❝ *When I get in a situation like that, I can't see anything but the flag; it's like a tunnel between me and the hole.* ❞

teams; in 1983 Wadkins dropped a thunderbolt on the European team on the last hole, a stroke that gave the United States a narrow victory.

Wadkins was matched with the Spaniard José-Maria Canizares on the final day, and Canizares was giving Wadkins all the fight he wanted. On the 16th hole the Spaniard saved his par after hitting a ball into the water while Wadkins was missing a birdie putt of 12 feet that would have drawn him level. At the next hole, a par three, Wadkins had to hole a six-footer to save a par and stay alive. He did, but Canizares still led by one hole. As they moved to the 18th, a long par five with water on the right, word came from Jack Nicklaus, the team captain, that the Ryder Cup had come down to Wadkins and Canizares. Theirs was the only match in doubt and if Wadkins could win the hole, and thus

halve Canizares, the Americans would win by $14^{1}/_{2}$ points to $13^{1}/_{2}$, the narrowest possible winning margin.

Lanny hit a good drive, then tore into a 3-wood, cutting across the water, and landed within 75 yards of the green. Canizares's third shot reached the fringe at the front of the green, 30 feet from the cup, cut into a little rise on the back left. The Spaniard would surely make his par, Wadkins thought.

Lanny's teammates surrounded him now, calling encouragement as he sized up the shot. His ball was below the level of the green, hiding the cup from view, although he knew what was back there.

"I've never been so nervous," Wadkins said. "When the pressure's on and you have to do things for yourself, you expect to do them; it's different when you have to do it for others."

All this must have flashed through his mind in an instant, because he wasted no time with the shot. He nipped the ball with a sand wedge, driving it for the flagstick. It skipped once, then grabbed by the hole. "I knew from the crowd's reaction that it was stiff and I raced over to see how close. It was about a foot away." His teammates mobbed him. Tom Kite slapped him on the back saying, "Way to go, Lanny." Wadkins tried to say something, but nothing would come out.

"It was an emotional moment. I'm glad I didn't have to stand over the putt very long," he said. The birdie was safe, and so was the Ryder Cup. "When I get in a situation like that, I can't see anything but the flag; it's like a tunnel between me and the hole," he said. "I've made some of my best shots when the heat's on, and that's satisfying, but this was special because of the situation. I'll never forget it."

Neither will Captain Nicklaus, who went out to the spot later, kneeled down and gratefully kissed the divot.

C.B.

BOBBY JONES

*approach to the 17th at Royal Lytham and St Anne's
in the 1926 British Open*

Americans had ruled the British Open since the Armistice ended the First World War. Roger Wethered, the great amateur, had tied Jock Hutchison in 1921, but he had lost the play-off. Walter Hagen had won in 1922, and while Arthur Havers had turned back the invaders in 1923, Hagen had repeated his success in 1924 and then Jim Barnes had followed in 1925.

Now it was 1926. The Americans had won the Walker Cup once again, Jess Sweetser had become the first native-born American to win the British Amateur, and in late June another strong contingent had come over for another go at the British Open. Hagen was back

Jones watches intently after a fairway wood.

again, along with Al Watrous, Wild Bill Mehlhorn, little Freddy McLeod, Emmett French, Tommy Armour (an American citizen by then) and the amateurs George Von Elm and Bobby Jones.

Only 24 years old, Jones nevertheless had already become an international celebrity. He had won the US Open three years earlier, and the US Amateur in both 1924 and 1925. He had played in the British Open of 1921, but had

picked up his ball during the third round and withdrawn. He was only 19 at the time; in the years that followed he had grown ashamed of what he had done. The 1926 Championship was his first British Open since that unfortunate day. Bobby had matured; he would never do it again.

He was playing superb golf. He had reached the quarter-finals of the British Amateur, losing to Andrew Jamieson by four and three, and after teaming with Watts Gunn, a clubmate at the Atlanta Athletic Club, in winning their Walker Cup foursomes by four and three, he devastated Cyril Tolley by 12 and 11 in the singles. Ironically, Jamieson had been Tolley's foursomes partner. Nobody beat Bobby twice.

Strong as these showings had been, his game peaked in the qualifying rounds for the British Open. Jones played two rounds at Sunningdale, a wonderful course on the outskirts of London, in 66 and 68 – a total of 134. Some considered these the best rounds of golf ever played, and Bernard Darwin called Jones's 66 "incredible and indecent." He made not one mistake, and his scorecard showed all threes and fours, not a five on it.

The Championship proper was played at Royal Lytham and St Anne's, an unprepossessing course set amid a residential neighborhood, with houses and a railway line close alongside, but with as strong a finish as any. Its 17th hole was particularly troublesome, 413 yards, bending left, with a succession of ugly bunkers lining the left side from short of the landing zone all the way to the green.

Jones had played rather well through the first 54 holes, shooting a pair of 72s and a 73, but when the last round began, he was trailing Watrous by two strokes. They were paired with one another and, after the morning round, had gone to the Majestic Hotel together for lunch and a rest before tackling Lytham in the afternoon.

Jones had been off his game in the morning round. He was putting poorly and he couldn't make up any ground on Watrous, even though he was outdriving him by yards. Hagen and Von Elm were close behind, but if Bobby couldn't catch Al, they didn't matter.

Rested by then, Jones and Watrous played evenly through the early holes in the afternoon, but Bobby stumbled toward the middle of the round, dropping a stroke at the 9th for the fourth consecutive time, three-putting the 11th and missing the 13th green. Watrous, though, was just as shaky; even

Bobby Jones's bunker on the 17th at Royal Lytham and St Anne's.

though Jones was doing nothing, he couldn't pull away and he still led by only two strokes with five holes to play.

Quickly, Bobby holed some putts and caught up, and they stood on the 17th tee level. If Bobby could birdie one of those last two holes, he'd have a chance. Driving first, he looked as if he had thrown away all his hopes. He must have come over the top as he moved into the shot, because the ball veered off into the left rough, settling on a patch of bare, sandy ground. Watrous, meanwhile, threaded his ball down the middle and, with a clear shot, played his approach on to the green.

Jones was in trouble. Sandy dunes lay between his ball and the green, and from where he stood, he would have to play a medium iron to a target he couldn't see. He walked far out to the

right, nearly crossing the fairway, to take a look at what lay between him and the green, and saw he had to carry about 175 yards and stop the ball quickly once it reached the green, if indeed it did. Then there was the problem of his lie. While his ball lay cleanly, it was sitting atop loose sand; dig a trifle too deep and the shot would die quickly; make contact too high, and the ball wouldn't get there either.

Jones assessed the shot, chose a mashie-iron, the rough equivalent of a modern 4-iron, then lashed into the ball. The shot was flawless. The ball rose from the sand, climbed over the dunes and streaked for the target. It cleared the tangled grass and sand bunkers crowding against the green and settled inside Watrous's ball.

The gallery roared and Jones dashed on to the fairway to see where his ball lay.

Watrous, meanwhile, was shaken. He three-putted, Jones made his par, and instead of falling behind once again, he went to the last hole in front by a stroke. Watrous lost another there, and Bobby had him by two, shooting 74 for the round and 291 for the 72 holes. Watrous shot 78 and 293.

Walter Hagen was still on the course when Jones and Watrous finished, and came to the 18th with a chance to match Bobby if he could score an eagle. His approach, though, came down well wide of the hole, rolled over the green, and Walter made five, tying Watrous for second place.

The Royal Lytham and St Anne's members never forgot that incredible shot and, like everyone else, they looked at Jones as a close friend and hero. His portrait hangs in a big room on the upper floor of the clubhouse and a bronze plaque stands where he played that magnificent and unforgettable stroke.

R.S.

BEN CRENSHAW

putt on the 14th at Augusta in the 1984 US Masters

The traditions that have grown up around the US Masters are more than the dusty memories of old Freddie McLeods and Gene Sarazens, and the sturdy legends of Snead and Demaret and Palmer. These have to do with the Augusta National golf course itself, of how its holes are shaped and how they are laid into the contours of the land.

Alister Mackenzie and Bob Jones, the designers of Augusta National, knew a thing or two about the game. They understood the situations that compel a great player to bring all his capacities to bear and they seem to have shared an instinct for the features most likely to inspire the critical moment. If they were after drama, they succeeded, probably more than they dreamed they might.

These great moments have occurred most often on the second nine, a glorious stretch of holes which puts forth temptation in its most beautiful guise and then exposes a man's weakness, be it his composure, his judgment or his courage.

Surely no one appreciates this more than Ben Crenshaw, who has such a keen interest in the history and traditions of the game, and who had always yearned to win at Augusta. Those who watched his performance there and found him such a sympathetic character felt it was only a matter of time before he won. Popular sentiment seldom enters into the equation at Augusta, but when Crenshaw's time came, as it did in 1984, there could not have been a single witness who did not feel a sense of approval and satisfaction.

Crenshaw's flaw is width, not length. His adventurous swing, which, in his own words, "puts me in more precarious positions than anyone", was under control that week and he was, as he usually was, holing out from everywhere with the most envied putting stroke in the game.

Ben climbed into the lead after birdieing the 8th and 9th holes in the final round, but he knew the real test was to come. Gil Morgan and David Edwards had mounted a late rush, and Tom Watson was closing in.

The players believe, with justification, that the Masters begins only when they reach those final nine holes; until then they have been jockeying for position. There, at the majestic 10th, Crenshaw holed a preposterous putt of nearly 70 feet. "It was absolutely off the

Below and opposite, putting with a touch of genius gave Ben Crenshaw victory in the 1984 US Masters.

The putt at 14 was a nightmare. The other one was a dream.

charts," he said. "After it went in, I began to think it might be my day."

A cautious bogey at the 11th, a brave birdie at the dreaded 12th and then a careful par at the 13th. A poor tee shot at the 14th put him behind some trees, forcing him to play a hooked approach that came off well enough but carried too far and stayed on top of the viciously contoured green. The 14th green is a horrid business that must be seen to appreciate what Crenshaw faced now. His ball lay 90 feet from the hole and would have to run severely downhill across a bewildering array of humps and mounds.

Even for a putter of Crenshaw's reputation, the odds favored his putting the ball off the green. Ever so delicately he stroked his ball – and the putt died 18 feet short of the hole.

Now he looked at another downhill putt, but this one would break sharply, and more than once. Only a holed putt could stop the ball from rolling past the cup. If he missed, Crenshaw thought to himself, a six was not out of the question and his advantage would be gone.

He could sense the Tournament balanced on the treacherous slopes before him. "It was a devil of a putt, but I could see what I had to do. I knew this was the critical stroke," Crenshaw said. Another careful glance at the line and the putt was away. It broke left, ran across a little shelf, then over a soft hump and, just before it died, it gathered speed, swerved hard left and dived into the hole. He had done it.

Crenshaw finished with 68 and a total of 277, two strokes ahead of Watson. When he was asked to compare the two long putts he had holed at the 10th and the 14th, he smiled and said: "The putt at 14 was a nightmare. The other one was a dream." For Crenshaw, and the Masters Tournament, another dream come true.

C.B.

BEN HOGAN

2-iron to the 10th at Oakland Hills in the 1951 US Open

Attacking play was Ben Hogan's strategy for dealing with Robert Trent Jones's redesigned Oakland Hills.

Oakland Hills had been revised for the 1951 US Open, whether for better or worse was a matter of opinion. Ben Hogan thought it was for the worse. All his life, he said, a golfer strives for length and control so he can place his shots. When the hole is cut on the left side of the green, with bunkers guarding the direct approach, the smart golfer will try to drive to the right side and set up a better shot at the pin – not at the green, but at the pin. He gambles that by playing close to the right edge of the fairway he'll have a clear shot at the hole. Hogan claimed he couldn't do this at Oakland Hills.

Located in the northerly suburbs of Detroit, the course had been built early in the century and had already been the scene of two previous Opens: the 1924 Championship, won by Cyril Walker, and the 1937 renewal, won by Ralph Guldahl. The members felt it had fallen out of date by the 1950s, and brought in

Robert Trent Jones, the golf course architect, to strengthen it for the 1951 Open.

Jones was a great admirer of Donald Ross, the man who had created Oakland Hills, and he believed no one designed better greens, so when he was called in to bring Oakland Hills up to date, he wouldn't touch the greens. However, he tightened the approaches by creating more bunkers, and pinched in the fairways by filling in the old bunkers 200 to 220 yards from the tees, moving them to 230 to 260 yards out and placing them on both sides. The openings between them were barely wide enough for a ball to fit through, and even beyond them the fairways were hardly wider than bridle paths. He did shorten a few holes, but this turned mild par five holes of less than 500 yards into brutish par fours of more than 450 yards.

He turned Oakland Hills into a terror, the most difficult of all Open courses,

the one others are compared to. No one attacked; it demanded defensive golf. Even the long hitters couldn't carry the new bunkers and instead laid up short of them, often driving with fairway woods, sometimes with irons, creating longer, often impossible approaches to the greens. Consequently, only Dave Douglas and Johnny Bulla managed par rounds over the first 36 holes. Watching the carnage, Walter Hagen grumbled, "The course is playing the players instead of the players playing the course."

Not even Hogan, the greatest attacking player of his time, challenged Oakland Hills. Going for his third US Open (he had won in 1948 and 1950), he opened with 76 and added 73 in the second round. At 149, he stood five strokes behind Bobby Locke, whose 144 led Douglas by one stroke. More important, fifteen players stood between him and first place.

Leaving Oakland Hills after the second round, Hogan told reporters, "I'd have to be Houdini to win now. I'd need 140, and how can anybody shoot 140 on this course?"

Hogan diagnosed the golf course once again while he soaked his legs in a hot tub the next morning. Obviously caution didn't work; he decided he would do what he did best – he'd attack. He shot 71 in the morning round, one stroke over par, and passed ten men. With a score of 220 for 54 holes, he stood within two strokes of Jimmy Demaret, the new leader. Demaret stood at 218, eight strokes over par.

Within striking distance now, Hogan was grim as he entered the clubhouse for a quick lunch before the afternoon's closing round. He had had the course beaten, but he had let a great round slip away, losing one stroke on the 14th, two more on the 15th, and missing a four-foot putt on the 17th.

I'd have to be Houdini to win now. I'd need 140, and how can anybody shoot 140 on this course?

BEN HOGAN | 61

Stepping on to the first tee in the afternoon, Hogan told Ike Grainger, the referee, "I'm going to burn it up." He didn't at first; instead he played the first nine in 35, even par, and now he moved to the second nine.

The 10th hole was probably the most demanding on the course. It had been

Standing beside his ball, Hogan sized up his next shot. The flagstick was set in the far right rear, and to reach it he would have to play either over or around a deep greenside bunker on the right. He had one break; since the green broke from left to right, he could shade the left edge of the bunker, avoid the

Hogan at the last hole, having tamed "the monster".

tough enough before Jones had made it so tight. Bobby Jones never could play it; three times in 1924 he had taken six, and he had finished second. It had yielded only three birdies through the first three rounds in 1951. Henry Picard played it four times without making one par, and Locke had made six in the morning, costing him the lead.

The hole measured 448 yards. One fairway bunker was set about 230 yards out on the right, and two more squeezed in the fairway at 270 yards, creating a narrow walkway barely wide enough to edge through. The entrance to the green was narrower still, closed off by more bunkers.

Hogan had made his fours in the first three rounds, and now he ripped a drive 260 yards, steering clear of the first fairway bunker and pulling up short of the second set. He still had a man-sized shot left, played from a shallow valley to a green set above fairway level.

trouble and still have his ball run toward the hole. He had one other advantage. No one ever played long irons better than Hogan.

Hogan took his 2-iron and went through his usual routine: feet set firmly, a waggle or two, then the quick backswing and strong thrust through the ball. It streaked off his clubface, cleared the left edge of the bunker, settled on to the green and rolled within two and a half feet of the cup.

"It was my best shot of the Tournament," he said later. "It went exactly as I played it, every inch of the way. I had a chance to win and I had to play well on the back nine."

Indeed he did. He holed his putt, played the home nine in 32, rolling in a putt of 15 feet on the 18th, shot 67 for the round and, as he said at the presentation ceremony, "brought this course, this monster, to its knees."

R.S.

GARY PLAYER

3-wood to the 14th at Carnoustie in the 1968 British Open

Expressive and determined, Gary Player gave no quarter in his battle with Jack Nicklaus for the 1968 British Open.

With its flattish, dull surroundings, Carnoustie is set on the linksland beside the Firth of Tay with all the harshness and mean-spirited delight the Scots so love in their golfing landscapes. Perhaps it is not the fairest setting in golf, but it is as fair a test as any, and surely the most exacting in the land. If it favors anyone, it tends to favor the player with the tenacity to keep coming and the wits to know when to strike boldly, as Gary Player did in 1968.

Carnoustie measured 7,252 yards for the British Open, which was being conducted in weather described by the writer Ben Wright as "seasonably vile". A cold easterly wind blew in from the North Sea, reducing the operation to a relentless slog. The Championship

eventually came to be disputed by four players: Gary Player, Bob Charles, Jack Nicklaus – all former British Open winners – and Bill Casper, at that time the leading player on the American tour.

By the time Player and Nicklaus had reached the 14th in the final round, Player was tied with Casper and Charles, who were playing ahead of him, with Nicklaus trailing by two strokes. The 14th is a par five, not long, but a hard pull, because it is played directly into the strong, blustery wind. To reach the green, one must pass over a ridge before the green, into which are set two catching bunkers known as "The Spectacles".

Player drove his ball well into the fairway, but Nicklaus was far off line and in the deep rough. Believing he was away,

Above, the eyes of "The Spectacles" at Carnoustie's 14th. Right, Player is elated as he sinks a monster putt.

Player prepared to hit his second when an official stopped him, indicating that Nicklaus was away. Playing a wooden club from the heavy grass as only he could, Jack delivered a smashing blow that nearly reached the green. A roar went up from the gallery; he had only a chip and a putt for birdie. Surely this was the moment when Jack would assert himself and begin to squash the opposition.

The interruption did not seem to distract Player; few men have been as tenacious as he, and never more so than when he was cornered. Staring toward the green, he could barely make out the flag whipping in the wind. He took out his 3-wood, gave the ball a great thrash and sent it straight at "The Spectacles".

Together again, Player and Open trophy are reunited after a gap of nine years.

❛ *Staring toward the green, he could barely make out the flag whipping in the wind.* ❜

Over the ridge it flew, toward the green lying 230 yards away.

"I was just hoping to hit it solidly so the ball would draw," Player recalled later, "and then I might reach the edge of the green. But it came right out of the screws."

Player's ball tore through the wind and ran on to the green, stopping 14 inches from the hole. The spectators who had cheered at Nicklaus's shot were now dancing, with their hands held inches apart above their heads.

An eagle for Player, to trump Nicklaus's birdie. Nicklaus acknowledged later that this was the killing stroke. It put Gary three strokes ahead with four holes to play.

"I thought at the time I should be able to hang on to the lead, but as it happened I beat Jack by only one stroke," Player says.

It was a brave, resolute performance, one to match the relentless demands that are such a feature of Carnoustie, and earned him the second of his three British Open Championships.

When we see men like Player and Nicklaus play shots like these, we are always delighted and given to wonder where they come from. Don't bother to ask, because they don't know either. They will shrug and say, as Player did rather appealingly, "I wish I knew."

Strange, though, how they did it so often when the pressure was on, almost as if they were waiting for it.

C.B.

KEN VENTURI

chip on the 18th at Royal Birkdale in the 1965 Ryder Cup

The 18th at Royal Birkdale.

Opposite, Ken Venturi shows his mastery of the bunker shot.

When we see a Ballesteros applying his genius to an impossible shot, a Watson his mysterious alchemy to the short game, a Player or a Boros that marvelous touch from the sand, we can rejoice and still hold a little envy for the talent these men bring to the task.

Few men brought more skill to the special requirements of the short game than Ken Venturi. He could make the ball dance. If you wanted it to fly low and hop to the right, or sing through the air and skip to the left, you only had to ask. And did you want the shot to check up or run on a bit? Venturi has probably hit a hundred shots that belong in this collection, but one will illustrate his assurance and wizardry. He played it during the Ryder Cup Match of 1965, held that year at Royal Birkdale, in Southport, England.

The 18th at Birkdale is a long par four

covering 447 yards over rather lush linksland. During a foursome match Venturi and partner Tony Lema were locked in a close struggle with the British pair of Neil Coles, who some held to be Hogan's peer as a fine striker, and Bernard Hunt, a man capable of great bursts of scoring.

The Americans were one up with the 18th to play, but, after a good drive by Venturi, Lema hooked the team's second shot rather badly, leaving Ken behind a bunker some 50 yards from the flag. The British team reached the green with its second shot, although the ball lay a long way from the hole, and had reason to like their chances. Venturi had a frightening shot, neither a pitch nor a chip, but something in between. The bunker was flat but wide, the ball was down and the green was hard.

Byron Nelson, the captain of the American team, was standing nearby

watching the drama with more than a little interest. Beside him was Harold Wilson, the British Prime Minister, an enthusiastic golfer who was not entirely unhappy with the turn of events that had suddenly put American victory in doubt.

Leaning toward Nelson, the Prime Minister said, "No disrespect, but you seem to be in a spot of bother now. I shouldn't be surprised if we halved the match here. Your man looks to have an impossible shot."

Nelson, whose reputation as a fierce competitor was well earned, turned to Wilson and replied: "No disrespect, Prime Minister, but if I could pick one man to play this shot, it's the man playing it now."

Venturi knew a five would not be good enough. "We needed a four, so I had to take a chance with the bunker between me and the hole," he said.

He drew his sand wedge, an implement with very little bounce on its flange, specially fashioned so that Venturi could play the ball from tight, firm lies.

"Get it close," Lema offered lamely. Venturi nipped the ball well, hitting it low over the bunker with heavy spin, and watched it skip across the green and skid to a stop inches from the cup. With a grim smile widening across his face, Venturi turned to Lema and asked, "Is that close enough?"

Lema gulped, glanced toward the ball and croaked: "I don't know."

His putt went in, of course, and the Americans won the match and the Ryder Cup.

As Venturi slammed the wedge decisively into his bag, Nelson shot a triumphant look at the Prime Minister, who was not a man to be caught at a loss for words. "My, my, Mr Nelson," he clucked, "you certainly know your man."

C.B.

SEVE BALLESTEROS

8-iron at the 16th and chip at the 18th at Royal Lytham and St Anne's in the 1988 British Open

Matching length to accuracy: the Ballesteros swing in action.

I n the midst of a great round one expects to see fellows like Seve Ballesteros play any number of wonderful strokes, but on the final day of the 1988 British Open Championship at Royal Lytham and St Anne's, Ballesteros hit two shots that were beyond wonderful – they were decisive.

Seve's brilliance had carried him to the top levels of the game, some said the very top, but everyone didn't agree. His stature in the game had been questioned coming into the Championship. He hadn't won a major tournament in four years and his admirers were beginning to wonder if his temperament would ever match his talent.

After much wildness in his youth, Ballesteros had learned to cut down on his swing, reducing his enormous length to more human standards, but which of the long hitters – Snead, Nicklaus, Hogan – has not passed through this gate on his way to mastering the game?

In the Ballesteros swing the body is seen to be responding to the swing, rather than the reverse. As the club is taken away, Ballesteros is very particular in setting it in the correct spot at the top of the backswing. This leads to a freedom of swing that is a great factor in the astonishing accuracy he so often achieves. One has the impression, too, that this freedom allows him to bring his considerable powers of imagination to bear on his shots.

He would be called upon for his best during that final round, which had been delayed a day by rain. The South African Nicky Price led Ballesteros and Nick Faldo by two strokes, and all three would play the last round together.

Ballesteros trampled the easier first nine, shooting 31, but Price stood firm, with the look of a man determined to win. He had struck a magnificent 2-iron to within five feet of the hole at the par-five 7th, but Seve had covered this with a 5-iron that stopped six feet away. Both

All eyes are on Seve Ballesteros as
he chips the ball firmly at the
18th.

had eagled and it was clear that neither
man was in a mood to give ground. Ballesteros made three more birdies on the
incoming nine, offset by two bogeys,
and they came to the 16th level, at 10
under par.

It had been nine years since Ballesteros had won the Championship at
Lytham by birdieing this same hole from
the car park, an area now declared out-
of-bounds. Playing his 1-iron this time,
Seve drove cleanly down the middle,
leaving a shot of 135 yards to the flagstick, which was on the right side of the
green. With the wind blowing left-to-
right, he played an 8-iron almost perfectly, allowing the wind to carry the
ball into the flagstick. He nearly holed
the shot; his ball stopped two inches
from the cup. One could contemplate
murder for such powers. To his credit,
Price played a splendid shot from 125
yards that was hole high but 20 feet left
of the pin. He missed the putt.

With the easy tap-in, Ballesteros now
led by one stroke and it seemed that
once again the 16th had brought him to
the Championship. But it was not over
yet.

After matching pars at the 17th, they
came to the 412-yard 18th, whose
wrinkled fairway reaches toward the
red-brick clubhouse that rises close
behind the home green. Ballesteros
drove into the right rough, landing
160 yards from the green, whose
approaches are flanked by bunkers.
Then, using a 6-iron into a slight breeze,
he pulled his second shot too far to the
left and over the green. The door had
been opened wide for Price, who had
driven perfectly. Then he, too, pulled
his second, and although his ball stayed
on the green, it was a long way from the
hole.

Seve's ball lay 60 feet from the hole,
sitting down in an uneven lie with grass
leaning against it. Between his ball and
the green lay a shallow depression with

a tiny mound at the side.

Using his sand wedge, Ballesteros
gripped down the shaft almost to the
metal and took several practice swings.
He was concentration itself as he ad-
dressed the ball.

His hands carried the club no more
than waist high on the backswing before
he struck the ball firmly. Once on the
green, the ball settled into a smooth roll,
glided gently to the right and seemed
headed into the hole. As it died, it curled
round the edge of the hole and lipped
out.

... jubilation as victory is assured.

6 *One had to search back over many championships to recall a stroke played with such exquisite judgment, confidence and touch.* **9**

"Ah, what a great shot," breathed Jack Nicklaus in admiration as he watched from the television booth.

One had to search back over many championships to recall a stroke played with such exquisite judgment, confidence and touch. To Price, the opening now must have seemed no more than a crack. He had no choice; he went too boldly for the putt and ran it 10 feet past.

With the little putt of inches, the Championship was Seve's. He had done the last round in 65, and finished with a score of 273 to claim his third British Open.

Ballesteros paid tribute to Price, who

had scored 69 in the final round, and had given such a good account of himself. "It's a pity there is only one Champion," he said.

In explaining his strategy, he said: "I deliberately played to the left on the last hole because of all the trouble out there on the right, but I didn't intend to miss that far." This comment led to a smile or two, but when he added "the lie on the chip shot was very difficult," everyone burst into laughter. As though Ballesteros might find the slightest difficulty with such a shot, and at Royal Lytham of all places.

C.B.

BOB TOSKI

*4-iron to the 18th at the Havana Country Club
in the 1953 Havana Open*

What constitutes pressure? You might imagine that it takes more grit to play a winning shot for $100,000 than for $2,000 and, for the most part, you would be right. Yet, as we sometimes discover, pressure is as much in the mind of the man as in the importance of the occasion and it could be fairly argued that few men have felt more intensely the pressure to win than Bob Toski did in the Havana Open of 1953.

Some people think that Toski struck one of the great pressure shots in the 1954 World Open when he cut an 8-iron around a tree on the last hole to beat Jack Burke and Earl Stewart by a stroke and win the first $50,000 prize in golf. The World Open was a carnival-style extravaganza produced by Chicago entrepreneur George S. May at Tam O'Shanter, a course no longer in existence. Every major player was there except Hogan, who refused to wear shirts emblazoned with the player's name. The winner received an additional $50,000 in appearance fees, an unimaginable sum in those days. There was pressure, to be sure, but Toski believes that he played a more telling stroke in Havana.

Toski had joined the tour five years earlier, weighing in at about 116 pounds (52.6 kg) fully clothed, with a body so thin and light that his companions began calling him "Mouse". He looked frail, but nature had endowed him with superior hand-eye coordination and a wiry strength that astonished his rivals. He became one of the longest hitters – some said the longest – pound for pound, of his era. Nature had also seen fit to place within this tiny figure a big heart and a fiery competitive temperament.

As with so many emotional men whose instincts ride close to the surface, composure was the most elusive of the qualities Toski needed for success. Quite early in his career, Toski found himself playing in a group in front of Hogan, then the greatest player in the game. Hogan's group overtook Toski's at a long par-three hole just as Toski was preparing to hit. Toski glanced back and saw the great man, set his jaw and took a mighty swipe. He skied the ball horribly, no more than 100 yards in front of the tee. Hogan turned to a playing partner and muttered, "Who the hell was that?" Toski fled even before the ball had landed, utterly humiliated. He vowed then never to forget this lesson in composure.

In 1953 Toski had met and fallen in love with Lynn Stewart, a ravishing auburn-haired secretary and part-time model. They desperately wanted to get married, but Toski was nearly broke. He had not been winning and had less than $500 in cash when he arrived in Havana. If he could win the $2,000 first prize,

Bob Toski's game proved the importance of inner strength in surmounting physical shortcomings.

Toski won more than just prize money at Havana in 1953.

they decided, there would be a wedding. Toski played like a man possessed. When he came to the 72nd hole, he was tied for the lead with four others—Walter Burkemo, who would win the PGA Championship later that summer; the talented Al Besselink; a dangerous Pete Cooper, who played the Caribbean tour as though he owned it; and Freddie Haas, the man who had ended Byron Nelson's run of eleven victories back in 1945.

The 18th hole at Havana Country Club is a par-four of some 380 yards that dog-legs left around the clubhouse. To the left is the out-of-bounds, and tall palm trees line the fairway on the right. Toski pushed his tee shot and found himself in the 17th fairway behind a long picket of royal palms. His prospects suddenly looked more funereal than ceremonial, for even if he played safe, he did not favor his chances in a five-way play-off. He could think of nothing but finding a path through the trees and somehow contriving to reach the green. He found an opening, but he would have to aim at the gallery that

lined the fairway on the left, toward the out-of-bounds. At that moment Toski noticed the Florida senator George Smathers standing just there. If he aimed squarely at Smathers, he would have to slice the ball almost 40 yards.

Only Toski knew how desperate he was to win and why there was so much pressure to make the shot count. Well, faint heart never won fair lady. He sent a low 4-iron shot screaming through the trees, cutting it exquisitely, and just as it reached the center of the fairway it began bending and curved toward the hole. The ball soared on to the green and rolled to a stop two feet from the flagstick. To compose such a shot in the circumstances, and to bring it off, was splendid stuff and it hardly needs to be added that Toski managed to hole the putt for birdie and win by a single stroke. He had captured the $2,000 and the fair lady. And, if matters of the heart are all they are said to be, who can claim to have played such a stroke under pressure when the stakes were greater?

C.B.

BOB TWAY

sand shot at the 18th at Inverness in the 1986 US PGA

> ❜ *It had been a long, hard road back and I finally made it.* ❜

Exultation from Bob Tway as his bunker shot at the 18th finds the hole.

Imagine what it was like to be Greg Norman as he entered the 1986 US PGA Championship at Inverness Club in Toledo, Ohio. He was the leading money winner in golf, on his way to winning the Vardon Trophy, and had led all four major Championships after three rounds. He had won the British Open and he was about to win the US PGA.

But now here comes this tall, skinny fellow with Brillo for hair who lobs the ball into the hole from an unlikely place, near the final green, and then dances on your grave.

The author of the not-so-dastardly deed was Bob Tway, who was having a good year himself. He had come back from the oblivion of the Asian tour after years of failing to qualify for his US tour card and he had already won three tournaments in 1986.

Like many tall men, Tway tends to hunch over the ball and has trouble getting out of his own way as he swings through, but when the swing is working, he is long with the woods and crisp with the irons, and he putts very well indeed. He had been a top junior in the United States, an All-American three times at Oklahoma State University, and his initial failure to qualify for the tour had surprised many of those who had pronounced him a coming star. Now, at

the age of 27, he was fulfilling the promise.

The final round began on Sunday, with Norman and Tway paired together, but rain forced a suspension of play until the Monday. With nine holes to play, Norman led by four strokes, the same margin he had held over Tway at the end of the third round, but Tway made up all the strokes in the next eight holes. He had saved his pars with brilliant recoveries at both the 15th and 17th. The 18th is a short par four of 354 yards with a sea of bunkers swirling at the green.

Playing a 1-iron, Tway pushed his drive into the right rough and then, with the ball above his feet, he chopped his second into one of the small bunkers guarding the front of the green. Norman's approach hit the green, but his ball spun back into the heavy fringe.

Nearly everyone had expected Norman to win, and Tway's shot from the bunker looked unpromising because the slick putting surface sloped away from him and he could see only the top of the flagstick, 25 feet from his ball.

Opening the blade of his sand wedge, Tway sliced under the ball with a shallow cut. The ball cleared the bunker's high wall, landed gently on the fast green and curled softly into the hole.

Tway leaped and danced through the sand, his arms raised high, scarcely believing his luck. Climbing from the bunker, he punched the air once more and then waited for Norman's last stroke, one that, in truth, never had a chance. "It had been a long, hard road back and I finally made it," Tway said. He remained composed until his wife, Tammy, reached his side, sobbing. Tears were filling Tway's eyes by then, too, and for a while he could hardly speak. For Norman, it had been a bitter disappointment, but for Tway it had meant everything.

C.B.

ARNOLD PALMER

6-iron on the 15th at Royal Birkdale in the 1961 British Open

W hen Arnold Palmer was in a mood to shake the ground, he could do impossible things; and when he was in a desperate situation, no one could be more dangerous. He arrived at Royal Birkdale for the 1961 British Open bristling with the kind of impatience and purpose given to those fully confident of their powers. The itch was upon him, because even though he had won five tournaments that season, he had won neither the Masters nor the US Open.

Palmer had won the Masters and US Open in dramatic style a year earlier, and he had come to the British Open at St Andrews intending to win his third major Championship of the year. But he had finished second to Kel Nagle, the unflappable Australian, who had held off Palmer's last desperate charge. There was something else. Since 1933 only two Americans had won the British Open — Snead in 1946 and Hogan in 1953 — and Palmer, now the dominant American player, surely felt this call to national pride.

One does not force things in golf, but Arnold Palmer did. He gave the impression that he was happiest when he was called on to risk everything on a given occasion, and he was quite prepared to accept the consequences. His open, genuinely emotional approach to adversity endeared him so to the galleries and, without doubt, enabled him to attack golf courses with such apparent disregard for safety. There was not one of us who did not envy the man and wish secretly that we could play with such abandon.

Royal Birkdale is set amid tall sandhills near Southport, on the Lancashire coast north of Liverpool, open to the hard, fearsome winds off the Irish Sea, but the holes run through the valleys between the high dunes, protected rather more from the wind than one expects at a links course. That week the

❛ *People thought I was half-topping the ball, but it was the best way to keep the shots under the wind and straight.* ❜

weather came in like the Furies. The winds were so fierce that Palmer had used a 1-iron, choking down on the shaft, to play his shorter approach shots. "People thought I was half-topping the ball, but it was the best way to keep the shots under the wind and straight," Palmer explained.

Gales levelled tents and pavilions, forcing a suspension of Friday's third and fourth rounds until Saturday, when the weather was only slightly better. After the morning round, Palmer led Dai Rees of Wales by one stroke; by the middle

Dramatic recoveries were a feature of Palmer's play in the 1961 British Open.

of the afternoon round he was four strokes ahead. Still, the Welshman would not be shaken and eventually finished within a stroke of the winner.

If anything, Birkdale is a stern test of driving, with its rippling grassy wastes and clinging willow scrub, which enclose the fairways and hover close to the greens. The 15th is a par four that begins from a lonely platform raised above the surrounding links and bends away to the right toward a plateau green with several guardian bunkers in front. As Palmer mounted the tee, he gazed at

a bunker set into the turn, which marks the direct line for the hole. Trying for every advantage, he drove across the dogleg, but his ball climbed up into the wind and he grimaced as it drifted into the deep rough.

He found the ball nestled into a thick tangle of coarse grasses and the choking willow scrub. A five at this hole now seemed likely, even welcome, and six distinctly possible. To reach the green, Palmer would have to carry his shot more than 140 yards, but from that smothering lie could it be done?

Another course, another tournament, and Palmer sinks another putt.

Arnold's eyes took on the look of the doomed man determined to save himself at any cost. He could see nothing but the ball somehow soaring from this wretched lie and finding the distant target. When Arnold was in such a state, nothing within reach was safe.

His shoulders hunched as he tore into a 6-iron with everything he had, cutting a swathe through the undergrowth. Chunks of sod, grassy roots, twigs and unidentified animal parts exploded from the grass. The proportions of the divot were exaggerated only slightly by Dave Marr, who quipped, "It would feed Ewell Gibbons for a year. It was Caesar's Salad for ten." From the size of the divot alone, no one could give the ball much chance to clear the rough, but it did, and landed on the green rather softly, about 15 feet from the hole.

Palmer had expected nothing less. Then it was two putts for the par, a steady finish and Arnold had his first British Open Championship.

A plaque was installed to mark the great deed. You may, though, have to wander some distance from the fairway to find it because the hole is now the 16th, following a renovation of the course.

C.B.

BYRON NELSON

5-iron to the 18th at Augusta in the 1942 US Masters

When Byron Nelson came to the final hole of the 1942 US Masters, you could almost feel it coming. Something dreadful or something wonderful was about to happen. Both as it turned out. Nelson needed a four to tie Ben Hogan, who had been eight strokes behind after 36 holes, but now waited in the clubhouse with a score of 280. Only Nelson could catch him, and everyone wanted to see a showdown between these two.

Although their greatest days still lay ahead of them, Nelson and Hogan, along with Snead, were the men everyone feared. Nelson had already won the US Open, the US PGA and the Masters, and while Hogan had yet to win one of those, he had been the PGA's leading money-winner in 1940 and 1941.

Ben was a determined, implacable opponent, certain of his inner resources. Jimmy Demaret once said: "The only emotion Ben shows in defeat is surprise. You see, he expects to win."

And within Nelson burned a fierce, blinding rectitude that could not be stayed except by the man himself. The flame sometimes drove him to do things that could not be done.

One could not choose between them in the pure physical mastery of their shots. Hogan was longer, but Nelson was straighter. There was not a better long-iron player than Nelson, but Hogan was as good. Nelson would hole more crucial putts than anyone until Nicklaus came along, but who has been deadlier from 10 feet than Hogan? Both were scoring machines. When they made mistakes, it was news.

The 18th at Augusta bends around a tall pine forest that crowds close along its right flank, and it was there that the dreadful thing happened. Nelson's foot slipped as he swung, causing a high push that sent his ball deep into the forest. Byron could punch his ball out sideways, but that would leave him with a

The 18th at Augusta.

Preceding page, Byron Nelson approaching the peak of his powers in 1940.

wood or a long-iron to the green. As he looked around, he saw an opening above him that led through the branches but to the right of the green.

"You can nearly always escape if you have room to swing, and luckily I did," Nelson recalled, "but I had to hook the ball."

There he was, feet below the ball, making the hook easier to play, but needing first to steer the ball through the little window high above him. He judged the green to be 180 yards away.

"I hit a 5-iron solidly. It sailed through the opening and on to the green as pretty as you please," Nelson smiled, "and I damn near made three."

His putt, from close to 20 feet, just grazed the hole.

The 18-hole play-off the next day was

all one could hope to see from these two. Even the pros stayed to watch, something they rarely did. Playing immaculate golf, Hogan led by three strokes after five holes. He played the next 11 holes in one under par, but lost five strokes to Nelson. On and on they went, neither man giving an inch, with the issue in doubt until the last. It was blood-curdling stuff. Nelson finally won by one stroke, scoring 69 to Hogan's 70, and earning his second Masters. There have been memorable play-offs for the Masters, but none quite like this one.

Curiously, this was the only time in their careers, so parallel in every way, that Nelson and Hogan met in a play-off. If Nelson had not made his sensational shot through the branches, we would never have seen it.   C.B.

PETER THOMSON

4-wood to the 18th at Vintage in the 1985
Vintage Invitational

Peter Thomson hits his second shot to the 18th and victory is assured.

How well we love the great battle at the end between two resolute characters, paired together, both intent upon winning. Our affection for these occasions is never more readily given than when one great stroke is answered by another. One thinks of the spellbinding finish by Tom Watson and Jack Nicklaus at Turnberry in 1977, or the sensational duel of Don January and Jerry Barber at Olympia Fields in 1961. The stunning exchange between Arnold Palmer and Peter Thomson at the 1985 Vintage Invitational also springs to mind, played at that Masters-style event in the California desert as part of the enormously successful PGA Senior Tour.

The popularity of the PGA Senior Tour shouldn't surprise us, because the players who have become so familiar through the years have retained their zest for competition and are as capable as ever of rising to the great occasion, although perhaps not as often as once they did.

Paired together for the final round, Thomson and Palmer had been tied a stroke behind Gene Littler, the leader. Palmer had fallen behind in the early going, but then he reeled off four birdies in seven holes and jumped back into the race. Arnold had only a tap-in at the 16th to draw level with Thomson, but he made a careless stroke and missed. Thomson then birdied the 17th and took a two-stroke lead to the final hole.

The 18th at the Vintage is one of those tantalizing par five holes that can be reached in two strokes, but it is full of gamble, especially at the long and narrow green, where a deep gulch protects the right side. Palmer drove well to the left, placing his ball at the preferred angle for approaching the green, but it rolled into the rough, leaving him 245 yards to go. Thomson's drive, played to the center of the fairway, got a nice downhill nudge and rolled past Palmer's ball.

Arnold then played a stroke of genius, a 4-wood from a hanging lie, shaped perfectly to the contours of the hole. The ball hit short, bounded on to the green and ran to the back, stopping two feet from the cup. The gallery came to its feet, cheering this stunning, magnificent stroke, knowing that Palmer was certain to eagle the hole.

Relishing the moment, Peter Thomson raises his club in triumph.

❛ *It felt wonderful. It was the perfect answer to what appeared a trump card.* ❜

"Through the years, the one thing I've learned is, don't stop, there's always a chance," Palmer said. "I felt that maybe I could put some pressure on Thomson; if I made three and he made par, the game is still on."

Thomson's response was grander still. Out on the fairway he realized he must match Palmer's stroke or risk losing his grip on the tournament. "I was shocked by Arnold's shot," Peter said. "I thought I had the tournament in hand and it was a kick in the guts. But one goes on and tries."

Using a 4-wood, too, Thomson laid a beautiful, arching shot into the heart of the green. His ball carried across the corner of the deep hazard and rolled over the edge of the hole, stopping 20 feet past. "After I struck my shot, I knew it was good," Thomson said. "It felt wonderful. It was the perfect answer to what appeared a trump card."

Palmer agreed. "That 4-wood was one of the best shots I've hit in many a day," he said, "and then Peter came back with one of the finest shots I have seen in the circumstances. I must give him all the credit in the world."

Thomson putted boldly, perhaps too boldly. His ball ran six feet past the hole, and then he holed coming back. The birdie gave him a one-stroke victory.

No one watching that day is likely to forget either of these shots, or the way the two legends, not so grizzled after all, went after each other with such obvious relish. Thomson would go on to win 10 tournaments that year and become the Senior Tour's leading money-winner, with earnings of $386,700.

"At our age, we're just out for the fun and the pleasure of it," Thomson said. And surely a good part of the pleasure is to be found in the winning.

C.B.

SAM SNEAD

3-iron to the 18th at Riviera in the 1950 Los Angeles Open

Above, Sam Snead is all smiles after his victory in the 1950 Los Angeles Open.

Above right, the classic Snead swing.

Watching Sam Snead at practice is the greatest show in golf according to some purists. Others will tell you nothing could match the sight of Ben Hogan at work. To most, seeing the two of them in action during the middle decades of this century was enough to reveal the wonderful possibilities of golf.

They were nearly opposites in their methods. Hogan's swing was an urgent flash, his strokes executed with the swift, breathtaking assurance of a surgeon. His control was extraordinary; one had the impression that his strokes were a part of him, even to the end.

Snead took things more leisurely, giving the impression he was surer of the impact than others and willing to prolong the feeling of it. There was a sense of an easy gathering of power, assembled smoothly and then released only when Snead was ready.

How different they were, and yet how much alike in the results they achieved and in the admiration they aroused. Snead refused to watch Hogan's swing; he thought it too fast, too abrupt, and he was afraid it would put him off his rhythm. He paid attention to Hogan's shots, though, because results counted most to these two, which was clear to everyone as the US tour opened in 1950.

Like any other in those days, the year began with the Los Angeles Open, at the Riviera Country Club, but the circumstances were not ordinary. Ben had suffered his horrible car crash a year earlier and, with him absent, Snead had swept the tour clean, winning both the Masters and the PGA Championship, the Vardon trophy, and the money title, and he was voted player of the year.

Now Hogan was back, almost miraculously, playing his first tournament since his accident and choosing to return at one of his favorite courses, where he had won two previous Los Angeles Opens and the 1948 US Open. Because of these victories, Riviera was referred to as "Hogan's Alley".

Ben was walking painfully, but his swing was intact and he was scoring as well as ever. He did everything but win the Tournament, and many thought he had when he finished with a score of 280. Snead was still on the course when Hogan finished, needing birdies at the last two holes to tie. That was unlikely at Riviera.

But Snead holed a 20-foot putt and birdied the 17th, then moved to the 18th looking for another. The 18th at Riviera is one of the great finishing holes in American golf, a long, gradual ascent of 443 yards. It begins from a low tee, then rises to a plateau, and bends to the right past tall eucalyptus trees to a green punched into the base of a hill beneath a white, Spanish-style clubhouse. The hillside spreads along the left side, providing a natural amphitheater for galleries, who have come to expect sudden changes of fortune here.

Snead drove to the right center of the fairway, close to the eucalyptus trees and within 195 yards of the green. To shoot directly for the green, he would have to play a low screamer below the branches that drape over the fairway. "There was no way of stopping it on the fast putting surface," Snead recalled. He elected instead to cut a 3-iron around the trees. "The pin was back left, so the only chance I had to get close enough was to hit a little slider to the left edge of the green and let it bounce off the bank."

What could be simpler?

He shaped the shot to perfection. The ball landed just at the bottom of the bank, then bounced on to the green and rolled to within 14 feet of the hole. To force a play-off, Snead would have to hole a putt with a foot of left-to-right break.

Just as Sam settled over the ball, a spectator fell from a tree perched on the hillside, causing the crowd to gasp. Snead stepped away as the man rose, waved his arms and shouted, "It's OK. I'm all right."

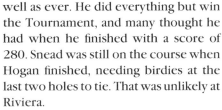

The greatest show in golf, according to some.

Sam Snead still going strong in
1983.

A wave of laughter swept through the gallery, clearing away the tension momentarily. Relaxed now, Snead returned to the putt.

"I was intent on making it and I didn't look up until it was nearly there," Sam recalled. "When I peeked, the ball was curling into the hole." As it did, the same spectator who had fallen from the tree yelled, then lost his balance and tumbled down the steep slope. "Here comes this guy screaming down the hill like a banshee and I didn't know what to do, except laugh."

Snead shot 66 and tied Hogan. The play-off was postponed for a week so the players could compete in the Bing Crosby Pro-Am, where Snead and three others tied for first place. Returning to Riviera, Snead played 69 to Hogan's 76.

"I got him pretty good in the play-off, but I think Ben was kinda tired," Sam admitted.

It had been a resolute performance by Hogan, earning him sympathy from the press and the public. It might have cheered some men, but not Ben, whose greatest satisfaction was found in winning. In this, too, Snead and Hogan were so much alike, as both of them well knew.

C.B.

LARRY NELSON

putt on the 16th at Oakmont in the 1983 US Open

The 1983 US Open was shaping up as another of those battles of the century. Tom Watson was riding atop the world of golf, winner of both the US and British Opens of 1982, leading US tour money-winner for four of the previous six years, and player of the year five of the last six. Jack Nicklaus was still around and still a threat – he might have won the 1982 US Open had Watson not holed that incredible shot from off the 17th green at Pebble Beach – but this battle of the century involved Watson and Seve Ballesteros. As it often does in these meetings, however, the victory went to neither man.

Ballesteros had not had much success in the US Open. Never the most reliable of drivers, he had strayed into the rough often, as indeed he did everywhere he played, but while he seemed able to recover on British Open courses, he couldn't handle US Open roughs (in general, American grasses are coarser than the fine-bladed British varieties). He seemed to become impatient and irritated when he should have remained calm.

The battle was to be fought over the Oakmont Country Club, a stern testing ground laid out over the rolling headlands above the Allegheny River, a few miles north of Pittsburgh. Oakmont is a harsh course that yields nothing and extracts severe penalties from those who try to take liberties and fail. It boasted more than 180 bunkers then, its greens were hard and impossibly fast, and its rough was particularly healthy and dense. Over his career, Nicklaus had probably hit more greens from the rough than anyone ever, but there even he often pitched back to the fairway after going astray.

Clearly this course would not suit Ballesteros, but he tried to adapt his game, driving with irons from the tees of even very long holes, like the 603-yard 12th, one of the longest in cham-

pionship golf. On the 2nd, for example, a little par four of 346 yards, he drove with a 5-iron to avoid a nest of fairway bunkers that crowd the right side of the fairway, then approached with an 8-iron.

Some believed that by avoiding his driver he had given up too much distance, but after 36 holes he lay two strokes off the lead, with 143, a stroke behind Watson, with 142. John Mahaffey and Joey Rasset shared first place, at 141, but they both played badly in the last two rounds, and when Ballesteros shot 69 and Watson 70, they went into the final eighteen holes sharing the lead at 212.

Larry Nelson, meanwhile, had moved into a tie for third by shooting 65 and as the last round began, he played the first nine in 33. Any other time he might have put pressure on the leaders, but he had actually lost ground. Playing behind him, Watson had gone out in 31 and opened his lead to three strokes over Nelson, who had passed Ballesteros.

Now, as they began the last nine, Watson lost his magic touch, and Nelson caught him on the 14th hole, where he lofted a lovely pitch a foot from the

Magnificent putting brought Larry Nelson the 1983 US Open and a record score for the last 36 holes.

Plenty of time for thought for Nelson in the 1983 US Open as storms interrupted the second and the final rounds.

Larry Nelson was bugged by an insect before he putted on the 16th green in the final round, but 60 feet later he was all smiles as the ball rattled into the cup.

hole, his fifth birdie of the Tournament.

A savage thunderstorm had flooded the course on Friday, interrupting the second round. As Nelson walked down the 15th and Watson approached the 14th, another storm broke. It was late in the day and when the rain persisted, the final round was suspended overnight. It would resume at 10 o'clock Monday morning, with Watson facing a 35-foot putt on the 14th, and Nelson looking at a 4-wood shot on to the 16th, an intimidating par three of 230 yards.

As play began, Nelson pulled his 4-wood on to the left side of the green, and Watson rapped his 35-footer a trifle too hard, running it four feet past the hole. He saved his par, but from where his ball lay, Nelson looked as if he would be lucky to get down in two.

He faced a putt of at least 60 feet, with a left-to-right break of four feet or more, and the putt would have to glide down two slopes. It was as tough a putt as anyone had faced in a critical position all week. Nelson studied the shot for a long time, then stepped up to his ball and stroked it firmly toward the hole.

The farther it rolled, the better it looked. As it drew closer to the hole and took the break, Nelson began to trot towards it, his eyes widening. And then it dropped. His mouth agape, Nelson broke into a gallop, chasing around the green with both fists held above his head, a wide grin splitting his face. He had gone ahead, and he had only two holes to play.

Nelson three-putted the 18th, but Watson bogeyed the 17th, and they finished a stroke apart, Nelson with 280, and Watson with 281. Nelson had shot 67 in the last round, completing the last 36 holes in 132, the best finish ever in a US Open, breaking the old record by four strokes, set by Gene Sarazen in 1932. That record had stood for 51 years; nothing lasts forever.

R.S.

Bobby Jones had reached the quarter-finals of the 1926 British Amateur, won both the British and US Opens, and then lost to George Von Elm in the final match of the Amateur. An idea was born: would it be possible to win all four in the same year? Perhaps. He would try in 1930, after his next trip to Britain for the Walker Cup Match.

In the meantime Bobby had defended his British Open Championship successfully, lowering the 72-hole record to 285 at St Andrews in 1927 and winning by six strokes over Englishmen Aubrey Boomer and Fred Robson, and later that season won his third US Amateur. He repeated his success the following year and in 1929 won the US Open a third time.

Now it was 1930 and the Walker Cup Match was scheduled for Royal St George's, at Sandwich. Appointed playing captain once again, Bobby teamed with Dr Oscar Willing in the foursomes and defeated Rex Hartley and Tony Torrance by 8 and 7, then destroyed Roger Wethered 9 and 8 in the singles.

Jones had played in two previous British Amateur Championships, losing in the fourth round in 1921 and in the sixth in 1926. The 1930 Championship would be the first step toward winning all four; he had to win to keep his dream alive. It was played over the Old Course at St Andrews, which Jones had come to love. Bobby won, struggling back to defeat fellow Walker Cupper George Voigt, who had him 2 down with five to play in the semi-finals, then Wethered in the final by 7 and 6. Along the way he also defeated Cyril Tolley, the defending British Amateur Champion, and Jimmy Johnston, the reigning US Amateur Champion.

With the British Open two weeks off, Jones took his wife, Mary, to Paris to celebrate. Before he was quite ready for it, the Championship was upon him, and he hurried to Hoylake. From the results of his qualifying rounds, it was clear Bobby was off form. He shot a reasonable 73 in the first round, but then came back with 77 in the second, calling it the worst he'd ever played in England. He would have to do better to complete the second leg of the Grand Slam.

Bobby shrugged off that loose round quickly, opening the Championship with 70, matching the course record, then 72. As well as he had played, he might have expected to be miles ahead of the field, but instead he held a bare one-stroke lead over Fred Robson. Horton Smith, another American, stood three strokes behind, and Archie Compston, a big, burly Englishman, lay five strokes behind.

Compston had beaten Walter Hagen by 18 and 17 in a 72-hole match two years earlier, and he began the third round at Hoylake as if he would bury Jones. He began 4–3–4–2 an hour after Bobby had started 4–5–6–3, shot 68 and moved into first place. As quickly as he rose, though, he fell, shooting 82 in the afternoon.

Bobby Jones in 1929, the year before he won the British Open at Hoylake.

The recovery that sealed victory
for Bobby Jones in the 1930
British Open at Hoylake.

Opposite, Greg Norman's
moment came in 1986 at the
British Open.

Jones, meanwhile, had gone out in 38, passing Compston, but Leo Diegel and Macdonald Smith were closing in. Now they were coming to the heart of Hoylake. While it begins easily enough, its finish is brutal. Its last five holes – two par fives and three par fours – cover 2,318 yards. Jones worked his way through the 14th and 15th holes without incident, but now he felt he needed a birdie on Hoylake's 16th, a 553-yard par five.

A solid drive put him in position to go for the green with his brassie, but the fairway bends right and to get home his shot would have to cross a portion of the practice field, which was out of bounds. Mis-hit the ball even slightly and it would be all over.

Jones didn't become the greatest golfer of his time by backing down from the difficult shot. He took out his brassie and met the ball cleanly. It cleared the range and bounced on to the green, but it rolled a trifle too far and settled into an awkward lie in a greenside bunker. Now he would have to play a delicate shot from a downhill lie in sand, and he might do well to make five.

Bobby hesitated a moment, then reached into his bag and drew out a strange looking instrument, a heavy iron club with a thick hickory shaft, a broad flange on the sole that rode through the sand rather than dug in, and a concave face that cradled the ball and flung it rather than hit it. This was among the first of the sand wedges; it had been given to him by Horton Smith early in the year, when they had played against one another in the Southeastern Open in Augusta, Georgia. Bobby had practiced with it, but he had never used the club in a tight situation like this. Would it work? He had to try; he felt he had no other club that would give him a better chance.

Jones took his stance, his right foot almost atop the back bank of the bunker, and his body bent low. He drew the club back slowly, then brought it down with a sharp descending blow. The ball popped up, cleared the bunker's front wall, carried on to the green and died two inches from the hole. The strange club had worked; he had his birdie.

Bobby played the last two holes in par, finished the round in 75, shot 291 and went into the clubhouse to wait for Diegel and Smith. He ordered a whiskey and soda, drank it quickly, then ordered another, trembling so he had to grip the glass with both hands. First Diegel faded and then Mac Smith came to the home hole needing an eagle two to tie. He missed.

When Smith's ball glided past the cup, Bobby took his left hand from the glass.

R.S.

SEIZING THE MOMENT

JACK NICKLAUS

1-iron to the 18th at Baltusrol in the 1967 US Open

❝ *Jack tore into the shot with everything he had. The ball streaked toward the flagstick . . .* ❞

Nineteen years had passed since 1948, when Ben Hogan had set the US Open scoring record at 276. It had been in danger only once; Arnold Palmer had threatened to break it at the Olympic Club, in San Francisco, in 1966, but in going for the record Arnold had taken his eye off the main prize. He not only fell two strokes short of Hogan's score, but he also lost the Championship to Billy Casper in a play-off.

Now it was a year later and Palmer was locked in another spirited battle for the US Open, played at the Baltusrol Golf Club, in Springfield, New Jersey, within sight of Manhattan's towers.

He and Jack Nicklaus had gone into the fourth round tied with Casper at 210, a stroke behind the amateur Marty Fleckman, but Fleckman drove out of bounds on the second hole and fell out of the race, and Casper made too many early mistakes. By the end of nine holes only Palmer and Nicklaus mattered, and even Palmer was dropping behind. Nicklaus had run off five birdies in six holes, shot 31 on the first nine, with five threes and a two, and led Arnold by four strokes.

Now Hogan's record was surely in danger, for Jack needed 35 on the home nine to tie it, and 34 to shoot 275. With an unbalanced par of 34–36, Baltusrol closed with two par five holes, usually easy prey to golfers of this caliber.

Nicklaus lost a stroke at the 10th, but he made up for this mistake with two quick birdies at the 13th and 14th, then followed with pars at the next two. Now for the last two holes. Pars on both would equal Hogan's score, for only the record was at stake now, because Palmer was still four strokes behind.

Baltusrol's 17th is a mammoth hole of

The leaderboard tells the story as Jack Nicklaus surveys the result of his third shot to the 18th in the final round.

The scoreboard reads:

RD 4	U.S. OPEN	TOTAL
-4	NICKLAUS	-4
+1	PALMER	+1

The 18th at Baltusrol.

630 yards, the longest in championship golf. Palmer made his birdie four, but Nicklaus missed his putt and matched par. Now for the home hole.

Baltusrol's 18th begins from a high tee, runs downhill for perhaps 300 yards, then curves gently left and rises to a green guarded by bunkers and a belt of rough blocking its entrance. A brook runs along the left, hidden among a forest of pines, then swings to the right, widens into a small pond just as it breaks through the pines, then narrows and purls across the fairway. More trees line the right.

From tee to green, the hole measures 542 yards; Jack had played it with a driver and a 4-iron in the third round, but now, with the Open at stake, put his driver aside and for the sake of accuracy drove with a 1-iron.

"There was no way to lose if I made six or better," Nicklaus said later. "The trees on the right are thick, the left side was not too inviting."

Jack took every precaution to keep the ball in the fairway, but he pushed the shot off to the right beyond the gal-lery ropes and on to bare ground, where the massive galleries had worn away the grass. He had other problems as well. A television cable rising from the ground and wrapping on to a huge reel obstructed his stance. Of course he was given relief from this obstruction, but when he dropped his ball, it rolled closer to the hole; he would have to drop again. On his second drop it rolled on to bare ground once again.

With his ball in such a bad lie, Nick-laus would not chance trying to carry the stream and chose instead to play short with an 8-iron, which should leave him a medium iron to the green.

He hit the shot fat. The ball flew hardly any distance at all, dropped to the ground, then rolled a little. Now he lay perhaps 230 yards from the green. "How stupid can you be?" he said to Palmer.

To make his five now he would have to play a very long shot, perhaps a wood, for the ball would have to climb quite high to rise above the level of the green and have a chance to stop. Nicklaus chose his 1-iron again.

Jack tore into the shot with every-thing he had. The ball streaked toward the flagstick, climbed high above the green, cleared the rough and the bunk-ers, dug into the green and braked about 20 feet from the hole.

Now the Open was his; two putts would tie Hogan's record. Instead Jack holed his putt, shot 65 and lowered the 72-hole record to 275.

Ironically, Hogan, then 55, had been in the field and tied for 34th place. His position was not good enough to win an exemption from qualifying for 1968. He never played again.

This was Nicklaus's second US Open Championship. When he returned to Baltusrol 13 years later and won his fourth, he once again lowered the 72-hole record, shooting 272.

R.S.

JIMMY DEMARET

recovery from water on the 15th at Augusta in the 1947 US Masters

Above, Jimmy Demaret probably had the best hands in the game.

The water-guarded 15th green at Augusta.

With all due respect, the 15th hole at Augusta National should be stuffed, glassed over and locked away in the Smithsonian Institution. Not that there is anything wrong with the hole, mind you, but how do you play in a museum? A par five of 520 yards, with a broad pond across the front of its green, Augusta's 15th is a repository of historic golf shots: Gene Sarazen's double-eagle in 1935; Curtis Strange's mighty splash after a mis-hit 4-iron in 1985; Fuzzy Zoeller's even mightier splash, over the green and into the pond by the 16th; Bob Goalby's majestic 3-iron for an eagle in 1968; Seve Ballesteros's sickening 4-iron that fluttered into the water in 1986; the mammoth drives of Nicklaus and Weiskopf.

would be replayed on television screens around the world. Playing from shallow water is not particularly difficult for professional golfers, but this pond isn't shallow and its banks are steep. In going for the green with his second shot, Demaret had carried the pond, but his ball hit into the bank above it, rolled back and disappeared beneath the water.

Demaret crossed to the far side and peered into the lagoon. Seeing nothing alive, he removed a shoe and one sock and rolled up his trousers. He placed his right leg into the water, then climbed back ashore to remove the other shoe and sock. His playing companion was Byron Nelson, who wondered if Demaret's piano-shaped legs would support

The hole is a shrine of famous and infamous feats. You can not find a place to stand where someone hasn't played a legendary stroke. Not even in the water.

When he won the 1947 Masters, Jimmy Demaret played a shot from the pond in front of the green that today

his sturdy frame as he clambered back, both feet now in the water. The slope was just as steep under the water, and it was slippery. The ball was fairly deep and it could easily drop deeper. Under the rules, Demaret couldn't probe its depth or ground his club in

Above, Demaret could deal with sand as effectively as with water.

Right, Demaret was one of golf's snappiest dressers.

the hazard.

"I'll be careful," Demaret said. He did not think to add marvelous. Demaret had probably the best hands in the game, strong and thick, but with a feathery touch. With one foot in the water now, and one foot out, Demaret drew the club back and then drove the club into the water, well behind the ball. The wedge vanished, splashing both water and the ball forward. The shot came to rest four feet from the hole. Jimmy holed the putt for birdie four and went on to a 69, sharing the first round lead with Nelson.

Even though the stroke was played in the first round, it was an extraordinary one and it gave him a great push toward winning. He shot four under par over the next three rounds and finished with a score of 281. The two strokes he saved on the 15th were just the margin he needed to hold off Nelson and Frank Stranahan, who tied for second at 283.

This was Demaret's second Masters victory. He had won in 1940 – and he would win again in 1950 – becoming the first person to win three.

In the final round, over the course he had built, Bobby Jones scored 80, the first time he had shot this high in the Masters. He would not play again. Jones was more than the creator – he was the reason all the best players in the game wanted to play there, especially the younger ones eager to prove themselves.

Through the 1980s, this privileged preserve has had just three curators: Clifford Roberts, Bill Lane and, most recently, Hord Hardin. If early one morning Hardin should wander out to the 15th and find one of these youngsters lurking among the trees, glancing speculatively at the branches, he needn't be worried. The fellow is probably looking for a place to hit one of those shots that belong in the museum.

C.B.

SANDY LYLE

2-iron at the 14th hole at Royal St George's in the 1985 British Open

❝ *As often happens when the mind is cheered, he then holed the monstrous putt.* ❞

One can find no graceful explanation for the sudden horrors that visit us in golf, those dreadful moments when the mind goes blank, reason departs and feeling vanishes. We know them well, these pernicious devils; they can appear without warning, even when victory seems to be within grasp.

Consider the experience of Sandy Lyle, whose breakthrough victory in the 1985 British Open at Royal St George's, Sandwich, was tarnished by a bad shot at the 18th hole after he had played a wondrous stroke earlier in the round. His fluffed chip shot at the final green, that horrid little stab which saw the ball check and return accusingly to its owner, was almost too much to bear. After holing out, the mortified Lyle went away and hid until a radio message urged him to return and claim the Championship trophy.

The stroke that swung the Open his way came at the 14th, the par-five 'Suez Canal' hole, so named for the wide brook that crosses the fairway just beyond the 300 yard mark.

The hole is a daunting one, not so much for its length of 508 yards as for its arrangements. The fairway sweeps inland from the English Channel and the mouth of Pegwell Bay. The tee is set in the very corner of the course, close beneath the old clubhouse of neighboring Prince's Golf Club, where Gene Sarazen won the 1932 British Open Championship. The boundary wall between Prince's and St George's forms out-of-bounds on the right running the length of the hole, and a string of four bunkers guards the approach to the green on the left side.

As he neared the 14th hole in that final round, Lyle checked the leaderboard and knew he was in contention, though still some way behind the leaders.

The tournament had resembled a dance for the first three rounds. Christy O'Connor Jr had waltzed over the classic links the first day with a record score of 64. This bettered Henry Cotton's mark of 65, which had stood for over half a century and had given the name to the Dunlop 65 golf ball. Australian David Graham then made his move in the second round in what may have been his last chance to win the British Open.

By the end of the third round, West German Bernhard Langer had joined

The 14th at Royal St George's with Prince's abandoned clubhouse in the background.

Anxious moments for Sandy Lyle before he was crowned Champion.

Graham at the top of the leaderboard and looked a good bet to add this Open title to the Masters he had won earlier in the year. Lyle, at this stage, was a dispiriting three strokes behind the leaders. It hardly seemed likely that he would become the first British winner of the British Open since Tony Jacklin in 1969.

The weather, which had been stormy most of the week, had calmed somewhat for the final round, although the wind was still blowing strongly out to sea.

These blustery conditions seemed to suit the big Scot, who had played much of his early golf on the wind-harried Welsh border. Now, as he moved to the 14th, he was closing in on the leaders. He knew if he mis-hit, sending the ball over the boundary wall, his chances of the Championship would be finished. Carefully, he aimed his tee shot to the left side of the fairway.

6 *One can find no graceful explanation for the sudden horrors that visit us in golf, those dreadful moments when the mind goes blank, reason departs and feeling vanishes.* 9

"I was aware of the out-of-bounds on the right," recalls Lyle, "and knew if I hit over the boundary line my Open was finished, so I saw just where I was going to put my tee shot – on the left. I over-did it, though, and went a bit too far to the left; I think I turned my right hand over too quickly. The ball got a bad kick and went even further left, into the really deep rough."

The dune-grass hay surrounding the fairway was so thick that the strongest swing was sapped of its power, so dense that balls had been lost. Lyle found his ball in the tall, clinging hay.

" I could have had a go for the green, but it would have needed a miracle shot out of that rough and over the Suez Canal. I decided to lay up."

The decision proved correct. His wedge landed short of the Suez Canal, some 200 yards from the green. Lyle thought for a moment, then he chose a 2-iron and drilled the ball low, a bullet that bored a hole in the strong wind and carried on powerfully toward the target. It landed on the back of the green, at around 45 feet from the flag, a breathtaking display of power and control.

The stroke quite obviously heartened Lyle. As often happens when the mind is cheered, he then holed the monstrous putt, converting what had looked at one point like a bogey into a surprise birdie. Fully charged now, he birdied the next hole for the outright lead and gathered himself for the march home. His final round of 70, including the humiliating chip, gave him a one-stroke victory over Payne Stewart, who finished strongly with an impressive 68.

Neither time nor opinion can dim the memory of that glorious 2-iron ripping through the wind, nor the putt that followed it. The little horror at the end is best forgotten.

C.B./N.D.

DAVE MARR

9-iron to the 18th at Laurel Valley in the 1965 US PGA

estiny is a fickle companion, is it not? When the US PGA Championship came to Laurel Valley in 1965, Arnold Palmer was the clear sentimental choice. The course is located in Ligonier, Pennsylvania, Palmer's home ground, and the PGA Championship was the only one of the four major tournaments Palmer hadn't won.

Laurel Valley, one of the golf course architect Dick Wilson's best designs, is long and difficult. It favored Palmer's game. Surely the fates and circumstances would be kind and reward the great man's army of followers. They didn't; Arnold was never a threat. The Championship belonged to stylish, personable and irreverent Dave Marr, who shot a steely nerved 71 in the final round to beat Jack Nicklaus and Billy Casper by two strokes.

Marr had a silky smooth, almost elegant swing that produced shots of remarkable consistency. For several years he was reckoned the straightest driver on the professional tour. He was also one of its shortest hitters, but not many could match his work around the green. He was an assured craftsman from the sand – indeed, one of the best ever – and was a confident, often deadly putter.

The final hole at Laurel Valley is a long par four, normally a par five for members but shortened, if that is the word, to 460 yards for the PGA. The fairway dips into a little valley and then rises to a green guarded in front by a lake. Only the longest hitters could carry the ball far enough to reach the downslope and roll to the bottom of the hill, thus gaining an advantage. Short hitters like Marr could either risk approaching the green

The 18th at Laurel Valley.

Dave Marr was a short hitter, but was smooth and steady on the green.

with a fairway wood or play the second shot short of the water.

Marr arrived at this hole on Sunday's final round with a lead of two strokes over Nicklaus, with whom he was paired, and Casper, who had finished. A clear advantage, but hardly reassuring when the man pushing you is Nicklaus.

"If Jack played his best, I knew I couldn't beat him," Marr says candidly. "To have a chance, I would have to play as well as I could and hope he stubbed his toe. And he did, finally, missing a chip at the 11th that gave me an opening. I made a birdie, which put me two strokes ahead, but with Jack, anything could have happened. And it nearly did."

Victory in the 1965 US PGA Championship earned the personable Marr a Ryder Cup place the following year at Royal Birkdale.

bunker. Nicklaus's drive caught the downslope and rolled far beyond Marr's. Even so, Marr had no choice but to lay up short of the water with a 7-iron. Nicklaus pumped his second a fraction harder than he might have wished and it skipped over the back of the green.

As Marr surveyed his third shot he could see only the top of the flagstick 123 yards away, but not the hole. Unlike so many of us who tend to swing too forcefully, Marr's smooth action was most likely to cause him trouble when he swung too easily. He chose a 9-iron and resolved to hit the shot firmly. There was a crisp sound, the ball rose toward the green, hung momentarily and then dropped from sight.

A loud roar rose from the gallery and Marr glanced up at the television tower, where someone was holding his hands wide apart. The ball had landed just short of the flagstick and spun left, leaving a putt of no more than five feet straight uphill.

If Marr could do anything, he could putt, and he can hardly be faulted for feeling reassured when he saw Nicklaus's ball lying 80 feet from the hole.

"Jack had to chip it downhill from a bare lie, and chipping is not exactly the strongest part of his game," Marr recalls. Nicklaus was not finished; he played a marvelous stroke with perfect line and pace, one that looked to have every chance of going in.

"Damn, if he hasn't made it," Marr thought, the color draining from his face as the ball crept toward the hole. If it went in, Marr would have to sink his own putt to win. It didn't; Jack's ball rolled across the right edge of the hole, the high side, and stopped six inches away.

Relieved, Marr holed his putt. Destiny had smiled and, as usual, had chosen its own man.

C.B.

Marr had come to the 18th the day before needing a four for a 68, and had taken six. Now, if Nicklaus birdied and Marr bogeyed, they would tie. Marr swung carefully, perhaps too carefully, and pulled his drive into a fairway

NICK FALDO

🏌 *To have made a three at
the 11th after taking four
fives on that hole...* 🏌

On the first hole of the first round of golf he ever played, Nick Faldo hit a driver and a 3-wood on to the green of a 450-yard par four. He was 15 at the time. Men live their lives without ever playing two such shots as this.

He was a genuine prodigy. Three years after taking up the game, Nick won 11 amateur tournaments. He became a professional at 19, and a member of the Ryder Cup Team at 20. Then his rise sputtered, and he rebuilt his swing, turning a pronounced upright motion into a flatter movement. With this, Faldo became more consistent, and in 1987 he won the British Open.

Spring 1989 saw him going for the Masters Tournament, attacking those last frightening holes. He had played erratically through the early rounds, opening with 68, slipping to 73 in the second, and finally looking as if he had ruined his hopes by shooting 77 in the third. One of the late starters, he had had to return to the Augusta National Golf Club early on Sunday morning, the last day, to complete the last five holes of his third round, which had been interrupted late the previous evening because of heavy rains.

Faldo had switched from his usual putter to a bullseye, but after putting so poorly through the third round, he switched to a mallet-headed model. The new club worked wonderfully. He began by holing from 50 feet on the first, from 12 feet on the second, from 15 feet on the fourth, and from 20 feet on the seventh, all for birdies.

Out in 32, Nick was suddenly in the chase, and when others, like Ballesteros and Mike Reid, dropped behind with gambling shots that didn't come off, Faldo kept coming back, even though he too threw away some strokes. Two superb shots put him on the 13th green, setting up a marvelous finish of four birdies on the last six holes, including a

putt from 30 feet on the 17th.

Back in 33, Faldo had played Augusta in 65, and had put up a score of 283 for the 72 holes. Then he could only wait as first Greg Norman, then Ben Crenshaw and Scott Hoch came to the 18th needing par fours to tie. First Norman failed, then Crenshaw, but Hoch played a routine four, forcing a sudden-death play-off, beginning at the 10th hole.

Faldo butchered the 10th, but with the Masters in his hands, Hoch missed a putt of little more than two feet, and they moved to the 11th, a dangerous par four of 455 yards.

By now the light had almost gone, and the players were having trouble following the flight of the ball. It was clear this would have to be the last hole; someone would have to end it here, or both men would return the next day.

Nick had driven so badly on the 11th earlier in the day that he had no chance to go for the green and had made five. Here, though, he played a fine drive, to the right center of the fairway, with Hoch a bit longer and left of him.

Approaching his ball, Faldo found it about 200 yards short of the green, lying in casual water. He was allowed to walk it 15 steps to the right, his nearest point of relief, and with the Masters at stake, he played a wonderfully bold 3-iron that flew directly at the flagstick, carried onto the green, and pulled up about 25 feet short of the cup.

Hoch then missed the green by a good 10 yards. He pitched on, still well short of the hole, leaving him wondering if he could match Faldo's par.

Nick didn't give him a chance.

Crouching over his putt, Nick gave it a sharp rap. The ball raced towards the cup, then dived into the hole. A birdie three; he had come back and won the Masters, when it looked as if he had thrown it away with that sloppy third round. When it mattered, he had played as good a stroke as anyone could have

In the gloom of an Augusta evening, Nick Faldo holed the putt that won him the 1989 Masters Tournament.

played, under immense pressure, on one of the great occasions. It was difficult to determine which was the more testing shot, the putt, or the nerveless 3-iron that set it up.

Later in the evening, Faldo said, "To have made a three at the 11th after taking four fives on that hole ... " and his thought trailed off.

R.S.

FRANK STRANAHAN

9-iron to the 18th at Hoylake in the 1947 British Open

Frank Stranahan at Hoylake in 1947, out to beat Henry Cotton.

S ome golf shots are so startling in their audacity that they linger in the memory regardless of the outcome. It is one thing for a man to brave a long carry or knock a wooden club shot into the hole, but quite another to come to the final hole needing a full swing for the last stroke and then, with every intention that it shall go in, to play the shot exactly as he planned it. One did not expect such a stroke on the final hole of a British Open, nor that Frank Stranahan, the American amateur, would play it. But he did, before thousands of hostile spectators at Hoylake in 1947.

Stranahan was an unlikely candidate for several reasons. He was, of course, an amateur; his swing was somewhat mechanical, without the graceful touch one associates with the short-game artists; and he had a rather abrasive personality that had put him in disfavor with the British public. He had played in the British Amateur earlier in the year and had behaved boorishly toward his English opponent. Few of us can sympathize with the petulant man, and there was no sympathy in the hearts of the British spectators, who gave Stranahan a cold reception.

He did nothing to improve matters in an interview before the Championship began. "I was kind of a belligerent kid," Stranahan admits. "They asked if I thought Henry Cotton would win. 'No,' I said, 'I can beat Cotton.'"

That he was the heir to a fortune didn't help his image. As a rich man's son he had enjoyed every privilege. He was wealthy, blond and handsome, with Hollywood good looks, and he had developed a marvelous physique from weight-lifting and following a rigorous fitness program.

Stranahan wanted to become the best golfer in the game. He pursued his goal by challenging the likes of Sam Snead, Ben Hogan, and Harold (Jug) McSpaden in money matches. Improving gradually, he became a leading amateur in the United States and eventually won several professional tournaments. Earlier in 1947 he had finished second in the Greensboro (North Carolina) Open, and then joint runner-up to Jimmy Demaret in the Masters. He was eager to play in his first British Open.

By lunchtime between the third and fourth rounds Stranahan stood one stroke from the lead, which was shared by Fred Daly, Arthur Lees, Norman Von Nida, and Henry Cotton.

The crowd's sympathy was with Daly, a cheerful Irishman who had gone around steadily and had finished with 293. All the others had dropped away, except for Stranahan. Frank had birdied the par five 16th from a bunker and now he could tie Daly with a four at the difficult 17th, a 418-yard par four where the out-of-bounds crowds against the right side of the green, and a three at the 18th, a shorter par four of 395 yards.

He reached the 17th green in two, hitting a splendid 3-iron to within 35 feet. Two Americans joined him as he walked along the fairway – Vic Ghezzi, a former US PGA Champion, and Fred Corcoran, the promoter.

"Make the putt and you win it," Ghezzi growled. But Stranahan missed, and then he missed again coming back. A five, and surely now Daly could relax; Stranahan hadn't the remotest chance of making a two at the last hole.

Playing downwind, Stranahan hit a lovely drive to center fairway that left him 150 yards from the hole. Distraught, he walked all the way to the green, thinking of what might have been. "I was upset with myself," Stranahan recalled. "I figured it's all over, and this is my last stroke." Returning to his ball, he decided that with the wind behind him he needed only a 9-iron. Then he stopped and walked forward to study the green a second time. "Sure, I was trying to hole it," he remembered, "but the chances were one in a million."

The crowd waited now, perhaps wondering what the brash American was up to, and not much caring, as Stranahan marched back, pulled up the sleeves of his sweater and swung. The ball flew straight for the flagstick, landed on the green and followed the contours toward the hole. The cup seemed to grow wider as the ball slowed and drew near. When it stopped rolling, it lacked eight inches of falling in.

The stroke was so unexpected, so extraordinary, that the gallery surged forward, hoisted Stranahan aloft and

That shot changed my whole life in England. From that time on, I was welcomed there.

Abrasive and aggressive, Frank Stranahan (shown here at Sandwich) finally captured the hearts of the spectators with his brave finish in the 1947 British Open.

roared its appreciation. From scoundrel to hero in a single stroke. "That shot changed my whole life in England. It was one of the great moments for me. From then on, I was welcomed there."

Stranahan finished joint second, a performance he would repeat in 1953, when he was runner-up to Ben Hogan at Carnoustie. He would win the British Amateur twice, in 1948 and 1950. He couldn't win the US Amateur, but he

was chosen for three Walker Cup teams. He turned pro in 1955 and stopped playing in the early 1980s.

One question lingers almost as vividly as Stranahan's wonderful stroke. Would the gallery's response have been greater had the shot gone in? Perhaps, but sometimes a great effort is less poignant in reaching its goal than when coming so near to it.

C.B.

BERNHARD LANGER

Bernhard Langer may someday improve on the magical chip he played at the 10th hole at Muirfield Village, Ohio, a shot that went into the hole and set up a victory for him and Sandy Lyle in the 1987 Ryder cup matches. At the time, however, Langer called it "probably the greatest shot I have ever played."

Ordinarily, Langer is not moved to such extravagance. The West German is known for his tight lip; his uncharacteristic outburst on this occasion was the equivalent of another player falling emotionally to his knees, waving his arms in the air and then toppling into a bunker. In fact, as his chip shot fell in, Langer did just that.

From the start of the match, Europe's Ryder Cup team had been fighting to retain the cup they had won so convinc-

Double disappearing act from Bernhard Langer as first the ball vanishes down the hole and then (page 110) he vanishes down a bunker.

ingly at the Belfry, near Birmingham, two years before. This had ended a long string of convincing American victories going back to 1957, and the Americans were now determined to avoid losing the cup on their own soil for the first time.

The opening day had proved a disappointment for the hosts after a promising start, as Europe hammered them in the afternoon matches and took a 6–2 lead.

On the morning of the second day, Europe increased its lead to 8 1/2– 3 1/2 in the foursomes. This included a 2 and 1 victory by Lyle and Langer over Lanny Wadkins and Larry Nelson, the same pairing they would defeat in the afternoon. Langer's unexpected shot was to have a great bearing on the match because the Americans came charging back ferociously at the Europeans with a fine double birdie burst at the 16th and 17th holes.

The bunker from which an embarrassed Langer had to be helped by his Scots partner is one of a necklace of sand-traps guarding the 10th green. Langer's second shot on the 441-yard hole had gone into the beads of rough that interlace the bunkers. If Bernhard was worrying about his putting at this stage, this was surely the best way to stop it. A punch, a good follow-through, only a fraction of bite ... and the ball trickled in.

It was a near killer blow to the Americans, just the sort of stroke that had sunk European hopes on so many occasions in past Ryder Cup matches. Lyle took over the running at that point, birdieing the 12th hole and then carding a magnificent eagle at the 15th hole to put the Europeans three-up. The prospect for the visitors looked good.

The value of Langer's chip then showed itself as the Americans hung on tenaciously, refusing to concede defeat, with Wadkins making birdies at

❝ ... there is nothing like seeing the ball disappear down the hole.❞

the 16th and 17th to slice the European lead back to one. Langer, though, had the last word: an 8-iron from 150 yards to within a yard of the last hole to shut out the American challenge definitively.

If anything, the 8-iron was as remarkable as the chip at the 10th hole, but there is nothing like seeing the ball disappear down the hole.

European captain Tony Jacklin shook his head in disbelief at his side's eight-under-par score, the only sort of figures that could have kept Wadkins and Nelson from winning.

N.D.

CARY MIDDLECOFF

Fover all of the eager, dreary attempts to suggest otherwise, there is no evidence in a rather extensive literature that golf can be explained in physical terms. The greater part of the game, alas, is mental. It is a game in which the emotions battle the will and the intellect, and the outcome hangs on which of these will prevail. It is when the prize is there for the asking that the trials of golf are often most difficult. No one is more aware of this than Cary Middlecoff, and it was never more apparent than on the final green of the 1956 US Open.

The Championship had come to Oak Hill Country Club, a Donald Ross course in the leafy suburbs of Rochester, New York. A tall Southerner with a keen analytic mind and an engaging personality, Middlecoff had won the Open in 1949 at Medinah, near Chicago, and a year earlier had won the Masters rather easily.

He was considered the longest straight driver in the game, his irons were rifle shots and he was given to sensational streaks of putting. He was a wonderful player, but not to watch. He was nervous, fidgety and unbearably slow. Picture, if you will, the scientists who performed the first atomic experiments in Chicago withdrawing the rods from the nuclear pile inch by inch ever so slowly, prolonging the end ever so deliberately. Not so deliberately, though, as Middlecoff played. When finally he settled over the ball, it seemed an eternity before the swing began. Then, just at the top of the swing, there was another pause, rather longer than you might think possible, then a long powerful descent, a little dip of the knees and the ball shot away low, then rose until it floated down gently on to the green. This was grand striking, powerful and assured, so unlike the process that led up to it.

Reaching the 18th green during a practice round early in the week, Middlecoff had encountered one of those vexing little putts that drive otherwise sound golfers from the professional game. He had played a splendid approach to within five feet of the cup, which was cut into a little swale toward the right rear of the green. He stroked the putt confidently, but it slid away to the left. He tried again several times, missing each on the left.

Cary Middlecoff making a characteristically maddening preparation for his shot.

The putt was forgotten and once the Open was under way, Middlecoff played brilliantly. Despite scoring a seven in each of the first two rounds, he trailed Peter Thomson, the great Australian, by just two strokes, and Ben Hogan by one. On the final day, when the 50 survivors played two rounds, Middlecoff climbed into the lead with 70 in the morning, and had picked up three more strokes in the afternoon. Then he began to struggle, bogeying the 16th and 17th. The final hole now, a 449-yard par four with a chasm in front of the elevated green. Behind him, a stroke from the lead, were Hogan and Boros, the last pair one wanted to see with a chance to win.

Cary drove into the left rough and then pulled his approach to the left and short of the green, still in the rough. His third, with a pitching wedge, was firm and accurate, stopping four and a half feet from the hole, trickling into the same swale he had reached in the practice round.

As he stalked the green. Middlecoff saw the scar of the old cup just beyond the hole on what seemed a familiar line. "Damn," he asked himself, "could this break the same as the one I missed in practice?"

Middlecoff knew he must make the putt or face a play-off. He could hardly bring himself to aim the putt as far to the right as he knew he must. Finally, he did, then stroked the ball. It fell in, just at the left edge.

Middlecoff slumped, dangling his long arms, utterly drained. Only those who have been in this situation can know what it takes to hole a makeable putt that is made difficult by its uncertainty, and do it to win a major championship. Because the task is delicate, most of the weapons that serve us *in extremis* – brute force, fear, anger, haste – bring only harm. What is needed most is a gathering of one's nerves and the confidence to see it through. Of course, these are just the qualities that are most difficult to summon when the great prize is so near.

Middlecoff puts it less grandly: "It looked like a rattlesnake to me. It was absolutely the greatest shot I ever made."

C.B.

TOM WATSON

2-iron to the 18th at Royal Birkdale in the 1983 British Open

N o one had won British Opens at a faster rate than Tom Watson: with his victory at Royal Troon in 1982, he had won four in eight years. Only James Braid, of the sacred Great Triumvirate, had won at that pace – four championships from 1901 through 1908 – but he had needed another two years to win his fifth, and here was Watson in the thick of the struggle as the 1983 Championship entered its fourth round.

Watson had won first at Carnoustie in 1975, at Turnberry two years later and then at Muirfield in 1980, each in stirring

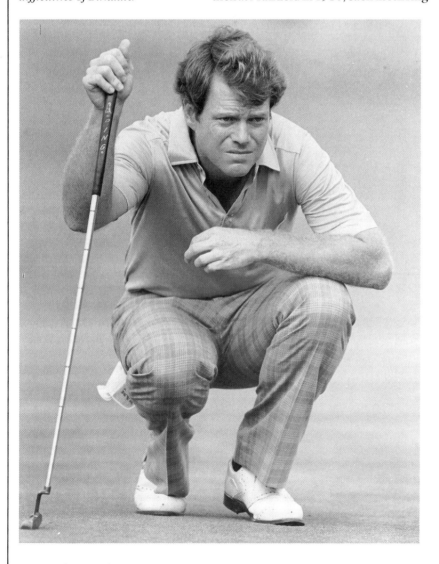

Tom Watson facing up to the difficulties of Birkdale.

battles, but Troon had not been a satisfying victory. He had shot 284 and had no hope of winning, since Nick Price had the Championship in hand with only a few holes to go, but Price butchered the 16th and fell into a tie for second place with Peter Oosterhuis, a stroke behind Watson.

Tom hadn't won a tournament in the intervening year, but he was still an intimidating presence, the game's most dangerous player on the big occasions.

The 1983 British Open was played at Royal Birkdale, on the west coast of England, a few miles north of Liverpool, where harsh winds blow in from the Irish Sea. A fairly young course, as those on the British Open rota go, Birkdale is a severe test of the game. Although the penalty for mis-hitting a shot can be savage, it is an honest course none the less, with all its problems laid out before you.

The weather had been bright and sunny all week, and record crowds had turned out. They had not been disappointed. In spite of its stern character, Birkdale had given up a number of good scores. Holing five consecutive birdie putts, Craig Stadler had ripped around in 64 in the first round, and Watson and Bill Rogers, the 1981 Champion, had shot 67s. Rogers had scored a double eagle on the 17th, a 526-yard par five, holing a full 1-iron. Then, on the second day, Denis Durnian, a professional from Manchester, had set a British Open record by playing the first nine in 28 strokes, six under par.

These had been some of the successes. There had been failures as well. Hale Irwin committed the most outrageous blunder, stubbing his putter on the 14th hole during the third round and failing to hole a one-inch putt. Watson had played the first three rounds in 205, one stroke better than Stadler, but towards the end of the day Irwin, Andy Bean, Lee Trevino and Raymond Floyd, along with Watson and Stadler, battled

Opposite, Tom Watson emerges from the melee after his second shot to the 18th.

"Well done, boss." Caddie Alfie Fyles congratulates his master on a fine accomplishment.

within two strokes of one another. At one stage five men had gone seven under par, but then Irwin and Bean broke free at eight under. It was a tight and tense struggle, with no one giving any quarter.

With the luxury of playing behind everyone else, and knowing what he needed, Watson caught up with Bean and Irwin, then passed them with a birdie on the 16th. Nine under par then, he hooked his drive badly on the 17th, but he fought back and made his par.

Standing on the 18th tee, he knew he led Bean and Irwin by one stroke, and needed a par four on the home hole to win. Stadler, who was paired with him, had fallen far behind on his way to a miserable 75.

Birkdale had been set up as tough as the R & A could make it. The rough was high and the fairways were so narrow that the players had complained they were afraid to use their drivers.

Responding to the criticism, Keith Mackenzie, the gruff Secretary of the R & A, snapped, "None of these fairways is less than 25 yards wide. This is the Open, not a monthly medal."

The field had backed up by then, causing delays between shots. Watson had to wait and had time to think about whether he should continue his nat-

urally aggressive style or play cautiously, trying to avoid trouble. The 18th had plenty. A long and straight par four of 473 yards, it was as hard a hole as Birkdale could offer, and its cramped fairway was pocked with bunkers. It might be time to use restraint.

Caution, however, had no part in Watson's nature. Even though he had driven into the rough on the 17th, he pulled out his driver once again and, showing complete confidence in his swing, lashed into the ball with all his might.

It shot off the face of his club, flew straight down the middle and pulled up about 260 yards from the tee, leaving him a little more than 210 yards to the green, into the light wind.

Again he had to wait, but once the green ahead lay open, Tom drew out his 2-iron and rifled the ball directly at the flagstick. It covered the pin from the moment it left the clubface, cleared all the waiting trouble, landed on the green, bounced twice, then checked about 15 feet short of the hole. Two putts and he had won his fifth British Open.

"I busted that 2-iron as well as I could hit it," he said.

David Graham had seen it, and said later, "I think those two shots were the best I've ever seen. He had such perfect rhythm, it looked to me as if he was playing a practice round. It was take the club out of the bag, step up, one-two-three-hit. Incredible. That's preparation. Watson was standing there inside a bubble, thinking about what he had to do, and he automatically did it."

Now Watson had won five British Opens in nine years, the fastest pace of anyone ever. He had matched two of the Great Triumvirate, for both Braid and J.H. Taylor had won five each, and so had Peter Thomson. Only Harry Vardon, the third member of the Triumvirate, with six victories, had won more.

R.S.

A fifth British Open title for Tom Watson.

BEN HOGAN

chip on the 5th at Carnoustie in the 1953 British Open

By 1953 no one could question that Ben Hogan was the greatest golfer of the age. He had won four US Opens, two US PGA Championships and two Masters Tournaments. Three times he had won two of them in the same year – the US Open and US PGA in 1948, and the Masters and the US Open in both 1951 and earlier in 1953.

Friends insisted, though, that his record wouldn't be complete without a British Open. All the game's greatest golfers had won it at least once – Bobby Jones, Walter Hagen, Harry Vardon, Gene Sarazen and even Sam Snead, Ben's greatest rival at that stage. Finally persuaded by Sarazen and Bobby Cruickshank, and by his own sense of history, Hogan entered.

The 1953 British Open was scheduled for Carnoustie, a public golf course in a grim, gray town in eastern Scotland,

Ben Hogan arrived at Carnoustie in 1953 with his eye firmly on the British Open trophy.

a few miles north of St Andrews and a few hundred yards from the North Sea. It is a links course, but the sea is out of sight, beyond an army firing range.

No one ever prepared for a golf tournament like Hogan. He had never played in Britain before, so he flew over two weeks early, found an ideal practice area at the Panmure Golf Club, just a short distance from Carnoustie, and learned to strike the small ball, picking it from the firm ground and tight lies, taking very little turf, as the great players of the past had done. He could have played the bigger American ball, but in a conversation with Frank Stranahan, the American amateur, he said, "I'm hitting the ball out of sight with my 2- and 3-irons. To play the American ball here would be a disadvantage. You've got to play the British ball."

The Scots were enchanted by his

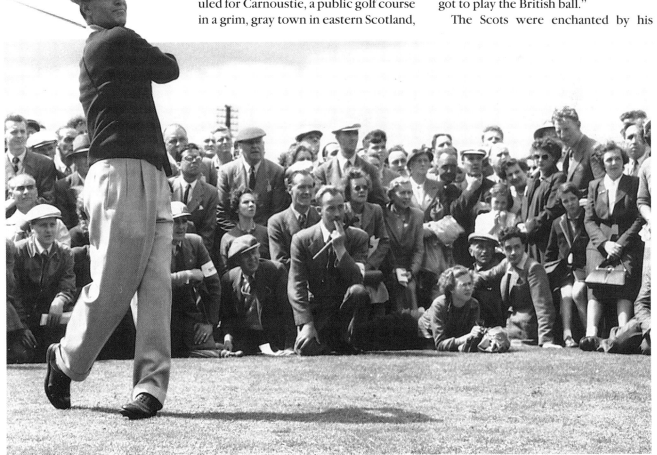

accuracy, watching him drop ball after ball at the feet of his caddie, who rarely took more than a step to either side. He also played Carnoustie frequently, often with Stranahan, learning its idiosyncrasies.

As an example, one afternoon he sent his caddie ahead to the green of the 6th hole, a strong par five with out-of-bounds all the way along the left, telling him he would play three shots with his 2-iron (Ben's 1-iron had been stolen immediately after the last round of the 1950 US Open and he hadn't replaced it). He would play one shot to the left front of the green, one to the center, the

third to the right front. The caddie was to tell him how each ball bounced. His preparation was meticulous.

The Championship was played Wednesday, Thursday and Friday in those days, with qualifying rounds on Monday and Tuesday. Hogan qualified easily, shot 73 and 71 in the first two rounds of the Championship, then 70 in the third. His 70 might have been two strokes lower, but he double-bogeyed the 17th, taking six, the only six he made throughout the 72 holes.

Going into the last round, Ben and Roberto De Vicenzo, the Argentinian, were tied for the lead at 214. The last

Hogan sinks a putt to birdie in qualification on the Burnside course.

round would be the decisive one.

Hogan had predicted he would need 283 to win; he must shoot 69 to make it. He began the last round with four consecutive fours, even par, and he reached the 5th hole realizing he would have to make some birdies or he wouldn't reach his target figure.

Carnoustie's 5th is a par four of 397 yards that begins over flattish ground, bends gently right around a fairway bunker, then runs to the green. Two pot bunkers stand short of the right side of the green, and two others crowd against the left. The green itself must reach 40 or 50 yards from front to back, divided into two terraces.

Hogan was driving the small ball 300 yards or more. Here he hit a powerful shot that cleared the bunker at the turn and left him only a pitch to the green. The hole was cut in the upper right portion of the green and Hogan was coming in from a slight angle from the right. He pulled the shot slightly; his ball came down about 18 feet left of the flagstick, caught the slope where the ground rises to the upper terrace and curled off the green toward one of the bunkers.

When he walked over, Ben saw it lying half in and half out of the sand, held up by only a few strands of grass.

Looking down, he debated what kind of shot he should play, whether he should explode the ball or try to nip it cleanly.

Ben had never liked to chip from sand – he felt this was the toughest shot in golf – but he looked across the green at the trash on the other side and told himself, "If I pitch over the green, I can just go to the airline office and get my ticket home. The grass is up to my backside and there's no way to get out of it. Besides, if I'm over there, I'd be pitching back to a downhill green."

He chose to chip the ball. He took his 9-iron, planted one foot in the sand, the other on the grassy bank, nipped the ball cleanly and sent it toward the hole. "As luck would have hit," he said later, "I hit it just right."

The ball streaked across the green, climbed the slope, sped toward the hole, hit the back of the cup, jumped three or four inches straight up, then dropped to the bottom of the hole. A birdie three where he might have made five.

One stroke ahead now, leading for the first time, he reached the turn in 34 and heard that De Vicenzo had shot 38, and that both Stranahan and the Welshman Dai Rees were in with 286. Par on the second nine would bring him in with 284. Instead, he shot another 34, breaking Carnoustie's course record. His 282 had bettered the previous best 72-hole score by eight strokes, and he won the Championship by four strokes over Stranahan, Rees, the Australian Peter Thomson, and Tony Cerda, another Argentinian.

Hogan never played in another British Open, but that one time was enough. Without that shot on the 5th, it might not have been so memorable.

R.S.

Meticulous preparation meant that Hogan got what he wanted: the 1953 British Open title.

BOB GOALBY

3-iron to the 15th at Augusta in the 1968 US Masters

The most vivid memory one has of the 1968 US Masters is that of Roberto De Vicenzo trudging from the officials' tent, numb and in despair, after being told of his scorekeeping error in signing a scorecard showing a five on the 17th hole instead of the four he actually made. That single mistake cost him the opportunity to meet Bob Goalby in a play-off the next day.

Instead, Goalby won and De Vicenzo placed second. To his eternal credit, De Vicenzo blamed only himself and pointed to Goalby's brave performance.

While everyone still talks of Roberto's mistake, the extraordinary manner of Goalby's winning is seldom mentioned or even remembered. A pity, really, because Goalby played with a brilliance and resolve that richly earned the victory. He had mastered the two most difficult problems that confront many golf professionals – himself and a fatal swing flaw.

A powerful man with a short fuse and a tendency to snap hook his shots when the heat is on, Goalby was a hardened professional by 1968, with great powers of recovery and an unyielding determination. He was toughest on and around the green. Perhaps he was not the most brilliant of putters, but his huge mallet-headed club was a feared weapon that had flattened scores of opponents when it mattered.

Goalby was rolling the ball well in the early rounds and he had conquered the hook that so often had forced him to drive with a 3-wood. A modification suggested by Johnny Revolta, a former PGA Champion who had turned to teaching, and a tip from Gene Littler just before the Masters began had straightened out his swing. At last Goalby was driving with the power and confidence to match his determination.

It was apparent, too, that he was playing his irons better than ever, especially the long-irons. Goalby struck two shots in the final round that were critical to his victory. He had driven poorly on the 18th and was forced to cut a 2-iron around the trees to reach the green. It was entirely against his natural tendencies to fade the ball, and he had a hook lie, but he managed it wonderfully, running the ball on to the green and making his par to close with 66. But it was an earlier stroke that Goalby and

Bob Goalby heads for a fighting victory in the 1968 US Masters.

others will remember best because it came at such a crucial time.

De Vicenzo had played the first three holes in four under par and was setting a blistering pace through that final round. Goalby came to the 15th ten under par, two strokes behind Roberto. Goalby hit a huge drive to the center of the fairway, leaving himself a shot of about 210 yards. The green was firmer than it now is and Goalby did not normally flight his long-irons in a high trajectory.

"I tended to hit it hot. You might say my trajectory was lower than most," Goalby says.

Still, he had a good lie, and if he could trust his new swing he was just the right distance for a 3-iron. His swing was perfect; the ball followed a classic arch toward the green, bit into the putting surface just to the right of the hole and checked up eight feet away. He holed the putt for an eagle, which tied him with De Vicenzo.

Both men finished with 66s and apparently tied, at 276, until the discovery that Roberto has signed for a 67.

"After that drive, I wasn't going to back off," Goalby recalls. "I needed a three and I was in a position to go for it. I guess that was the greatest shot I've hit under pressure."

Goalby had played in eight previous Masters with no indication he had the ability to win it. To win there, he told Bob Jones, was "the thrill of his life". Goalby still has the letter Jones wrote in reply, praising Goalby's bravery and composure, and singling out the 3-iron shot as "one of the greatest ever played to the 15th green."

To a veteran like Goalby, nothing could have meant more, coming, as it did, from a man like Jones.

C.B.

The view from the crest of the hill at Augusta's 15th, scene of Bob Goalby's great 3-iron shot.

FREDDY TAIT

*pitch from the bunker on the 17th at Prestwick
in the 1899 British Amateur Championship*

❦ *He was never beaten so long as there were holes to play.* ❦

Freddy Tait was a genuine Scottish hero, a dashing figure whose captivating personality and pure power were storybook stuff and whose love of competition and flair for turning defeat into victory made him a legend.

His father was for a time a professor of mathematics at Queen's College in Belfast, and once worked out the theory that a gutta percha ball could be driven no farther than 191 yards. His son tore that theory to shreds by driving the green of the 13th hole at St Andrews, a distance of 341 yards; the shot was said to have *carried* 250 yards.

Freddy played his first round of golf when he was 7 years old and improved steadily. Some of his scores were phenomenal. At 20 he became a member of the Royal and Ancient Golf Club of St Andrews and later in the year shot 77, the lowest an amateur had ever scored over the Old Course. In 1894 he shot 72, setting the course record. Later in the year he shot 72 at Carnoustie, which can be more punishing than the Old Course.

Freddy came along at the same time as the great John Ball and Harold Hilton, two of the very best amateurs Britain has produced. Born in 1870, Tait was seven years younger than Ball, and a year younger than Hilton. By the time Tait had won his first Amateur, in 1896, Ball had won four Amateur Championships and one Open, and Hilton had won the Open.

Freddy played a series of memorable matches with Ball, which reached their climax in the Amateur Championship of 1899, at Prestwick, the historic course that was the birthplace of the British Open.

Tait had not done well in 1897, when he was the defending Champion, losing in the third round. Now he was defending again, following his decisive victory over Hilton a year earlier.

He and Hilton came together in the quarter-finals. This was no replay of their meeting a year earlier, for Hilton fought Tait a tough, close battle. Although Hilton won two of the first three holes, Tait struggled back and won by laying Hilton a stymie on the last green.

The final match, against Ball, still ranks among the more gripping the Championship has seen, for here were two of the three best amateurs of their time playing for the biggest prize in golf, for in those times amateur golf was more important than professional golf.

For a time it looked as if Tait would handle Ball easily. He shot 79 in the forenoon, against Ball's 81, but he was not nearly so sharp after lunch and, hole by hole, Ball worked back into the match. Playing much the steadier golf, Ball had pulled even by the end of six holes, and moved ahead after the 13th, as Tait's game seemed to fall apart. It looked as if Ball might close out the match on the 17th, the dreaded Alps.

Here Tait mis-hit his second. His ball cleared the hill that blocks the green from sight, but he had underclubbed and it fell short and dropped into the broad and deep bunker that shuts off the entrance to the green. Adding to his troubles, the bunker was flooded from overnight rain and Tait's ball lay under water. Even though Ball had underclubbed as well, he had missed the flooded area by a few inches and had a reasonable chance for at worst a five. Tait, on the other hand, might make anything.

With the match at stake, Freddy had no choice but to play the shot. He waded into the pool and stood ankle deep studying what he had to do. It would have been a difficult shot even without the water, and there were no sand wedges in those days. Not only must he dig the ball out of the sand, he must also play it high enough to clear the front wall of the bunker, which was held up by railroad sleepers. The rules

Murky waters for Freddy Tait at the Alps at Prestwick.

then offered no relief from casual water, and Tait couldn't afford to drop outside the water at the cost of a stroke.

Most of the large gallery had gathered on the right, straining for a glimpse of what the great scrambler might do. Tait's caddie stood behind him, a step or two outside the water, and Ball stood across from him, on the wooden stairway leading from the bunker to the high ground beyond.

After a moment's hesitation, Tait flung himself into the shot. A plume of water flared up from his club and the ball popped out, cleared the sleepers and rolled on to the green.

The gallery roared, for in this one shot Tait had shown the spirit that had made him so heroic. He was never beaten so long as there were holes to play. He had played many great shots in his career, but few with more at stake.

Tait made his five, matching Ball, then won the 18th with a birdie three, sending the match into extra holes.

Ball was every bit as tough as Tait though, and he ended the match on the 37th with a birdie three, winning his fifth Amateur Championship.

Tait and Ball met again at Royal Lytham & St Anne's, in October. It was another classic, demonstrating Tait's great fighting spirit. Four down after 23 holes, he struggled back and defeated Ball on the 36th.

This was the last match Tait played. A graduate of Sandhurst and a member of the Black Watch regiment, he was shipped off to South Africa three weeks later. He fell in battle the following February, killed by a Boer bullet as he pushed ever forward, once again taking the fight to the enemy.

R.S.

GREG NORMAN

7-iron to the 14th at Turnberry in the 1986 British Open

It was rough at Turnberry in 1986 for the British Open Championship. The weather was rough – but most of all, the rough was *very* rough.

Tom Watson threatened to write a letter to the Royal and Ancient about the knee-high dune grass, gorse and heather surrounding the fairways – ribbon fairways, which he had even bothered to pace out sideways during practice. He found there was only one fairway on the Scottish course that had a width greater than the length of an English cricket pitch (22 yards).

Lee Trevino called the rough 'savage'. Craig Stadler carded a miserable 82 and then pulled out after saying he had sprained a wrist in the tough, grabbing grass.

Australian Greg Norman is a big man with a powerful strike. Even he had plenty to say about the Turnberry rough after the first round, a round that left

Below, rough times at Turnberry for Norman.

many a Championship hope in tatters. Norman, who had had his share of disappointments in several major championships already, wondered if he might sue the R & A if he injured himself in it. R & A Secretary Michael Bonallack was unsympathetic. He just said that players were not under an obligation to hit impossible shots in the rough – they could always take a drop under penalty. But Norman came to terms with Turnberry's rough.

That rough, which very early on ended the dreams of such as Watson, Sandy Lyle, the defending Champion, Seve Ballesteros, Ray Floyd – only weeks earlier the US Open Champion, Payne Stewart, Jack Nicklaus, and Lee Trevino, was also to provide one of the only really memorable and eventually telling shots in the Open. And it was Norman who produced it out of the jaws of uncertainty.

The shot was not, to a purist, that wondrous. It was a competently enough struck 7-iron, which rose out of the Turnberry patchwork of trampled heather and grass as if on a piece of elastic tied to the 14th flag. True, it had a deadly trajectory, which saw it arc in and actually strike the stick, finishing within simple holing distance for such an accomplished putter as Norman. But it was never an Open-winning shot. No, it was the knowledge that this time the big blond Shark was not going to let a major title slip from his grasp, the fact exemplified by the very determination of the pitch out of that heart-breaking rough. And to his opponents, who may have felt that they had just a glimmer of a hope that Norman might choke, it was the final death-knell to their British Open aspirations.

To grasp the significance of the shot, you have to remember that Norman had

Right, Greg Norman on line for his first major victory.

> The weather was rough – but most of all, the rough was very rough.

Above and opposite, Norman's recoveries from the rough saved him throughout the British Open.

❛I deliberately kept myself nervous before the last round by keeping thinking about winning. I didn't want to feel flat mentally ... ❜

already thrown away one great chance of a major title earlier in the year when he 'froze' on a 4-iron right at the crucial moment during the magnificent finale of Jack Nicklaus's Masters. And only weeks before, at the US Open, he allowed a one-shot lead after three rounds to deteriorate into a humbling 12th place.

As he fought his way around Turnberry, the thought of winning was always in his head – and he was certainly not afraid of it. A near-miraculous round of 63 on day two virtually won the British Open on its own. Only fleetingly did anyone look like catching him as the wind and rain carved up his lead after round three. His drives often found the rough, but his powers of recovery were described as 'quite exemplary' by one golfwriter.

And that was the important factor.

For Norman, when he arrived at the 14th, it was 'no worries'. With only

Englishman Gordon Brand to offer the most fragile of resistance, and a margin of five shots between the two, there was no pressure on him. As if to prove he had grown that extra few inches in stature, Norman delivered the execution blow.

The 14th at Turnberry is a troublesome 440-yarder with a dog-leg left line in. Right on the dog-leg halfway is a large bunker, which persuades many a drive to be pushed out of its reach. The rough awaits the drive only slightly off line and, sure enough, Norman's ball slid into the long grass at about 280 yards from the tee.

His approach now was around 160 yards on to a green guarded by three bunkers. With a strength of purpose he had not always shown in other major bids, Norman chose his 7-iron, clipped the ball out of the tangle of grass confidently, sweetly and surely, watching it settle to within tap-in distance from the hole.

There were no doubts now and Norman rounded off with a 69, five shots in front of surprise runner-up Gordon Brand, to become the first Australian to win the British Open since Peter Thomson in 1965.

Norman's words at the traditional post-Championship press conference seemed to confirm the self-confidence he had found at Turnberry. He said: "I deliberately kept myself nervous before the last round by keeping thinking about winning. I didn't want to feel flat mentally like I did in the last round of the US Open. And it worked. I played some great golf and hit some shots that even impressed myself, particularly with my irons. I played for the pin each time and they all seemed to go where I wanted them to. The best shot I played was the 7-iron I took out of the rough at the 14th, which hit the pin. I could not have asked for more."

N.D.

PETER THOMSON

*wedge to the 16th at Royal Birkdale in the 1954
British Open*

To Peter Thomson there is nothing very complicated about golf. You take the club back and swing it through, and don't forget to give the ball a smart spank as you do. The putting stroke is straight back and straight through, and mind that you aim at the hole. What could be simpler? Asked to write instruction books, Thomson always declined. What for? There isn't enough to say, surely not enough to fill a book. Besides, there are more interesting things in life. Thomson takes a keen interest in music, history and the classics, he writes as well as he plays and he is active in politics, rather more than his constituents feel is good for him.

Thomson had shown a liking for links golf while he was learning the game in

Peter Thomson made golf look a simple game as he won the first of his five British Open titles.

Australia and he had taken quite easily to British courses. In the British Open he had finished second to Bobby Locke in 1952 and to Hogan in 1953. As the 1954 Championship began at Royal Birkdale, Locke was favored to win once again. There was a great scramble for position through the first three rounds and, as the last round drew on, Thomson came to the 16th knowing he was one of four men in position to win.

Before Birkdale was remodelled, the

16th measured 510 yards. To reach the green with his second shot, Thomson had to play his ball through a gate of two bunkers lying before the green. It failed to get through. It caught the left bunker and lodged in soft sand under a lip of five feet. Peter was 25 yards from the flagstick on a steep upslope, and not very confident of his bunker play. "I was not a great practicer of the short game, and bunkers didn't seem important to me, because I kept out of them," Thomson

Peter Thomson had needed the bunker skills he demonstrated in this 1955 exhibition match to win the British Open a year earlier.

says. But he is not a man to dwell on things, which can be a great asset in golf.

Seizing his sand wedge, a Macgregor dual-purpose model designed by Toney Penna, he marched into the bunker. With no place to dig in on the steep slope, he stood with feet together, eyes clamped shut. "Lump in throat, heart in mouth, too. I was hoping to get out and land anywhere on the green," Thomson recalls.

Standing nearby, Norman Von Nida, Peter's Australian colleague, admitted later he couldn't bear to watch. Thomson exploded the ball; it flew high, arching perhaps 30 feet above the sand, landed on the green with a heavy plop and settled almost immediately. It lay within the width of a ball from the hole.

A sedate four and thank you very much.

"That stroke won for me, no doubt. Had I made a mess of that one, I'd have been a goner," Thomson says.

He won by one stroke from Locke, Syd Scott and Dai Rees. It was Thomson's first British Open, but not his last. He was to go on and win no fewer than four others.

Was there anything to be learned in this, one wanted to know?

"Well, you've got to be in good shape, it helps to be a little nervous, and you must have your wits about you." Nothing more than this? Ah, there would be. "Thereafter, I made sure to win by more than one stroke." And there ends the lesson by Thomson.

C.B.

TONY JACKLIN

driver on the 18th at Royal Lytham and St Anne's in the 1969 British Open

> ❝ *I remembered how many good players had lost the Championship here by making a six, but I decided I would not be cautious.* ❞

In 1988 Tony Jacklin played his first Open Championship for many years, a nostalgic return to Royal Lytham and St Anne's, the scene of his great triumph in 1969.

He was not to repeat that splendid deed of nearly two decades before, but the British gallery followed him back in time; they remembered when the shortest of putts and the bravest of drives won a British Open Championship.

Jacklin may have sensed that this would be his last appearance at storied Lytham and, with son Warren caddying proudly, Jacklin wiped away a tear as the crowd shouted out "good old Tony". They, and he, were remembering that emotional moment in 1969 when a Lincolnshire professional, filled with hope and talent, became the golden boy of British golf.

It was six years earlier than that, in

One of the most testing final tee shots in Championship golf faced Tony Jacklin in the 1969 British Open. Many players had failed to overcome its challenge but Jacklin rose to the occasion with a magnificent drive that gave the gallery its first British winner for 18 years.

1963, that Jacklin, the son of a lorry driver in a Scunthorpe steelworks, had turned professional. His talent was evident to all, but a number of persistent flaws remained in his game. He took time on the American tour in 1968, winning the Jacksonville Open, but equally importantly learning from his American rivals, and giving his own play greater consistency. This yielded no immediate results in terms of wins in 1969, but Jacklin arrived at Royal Lytham and St Anne's in a confident mood.

It was round about the 260-yard mark on the 18th hole where the crowd rose in 1988 to give Jacklin his acclaim, for this was the point to which he had driven 19 years earlier. That 260-yard drive was the blow that finally sealed the fate of Jacklin's only surviving rival for the British Open crown, New Zealand's Bob Charles.

Jacklin had built on his encouraging play before the British Open and posted scores of 68, 70 and 70 to take a two-shot lead after three rounds. His nearest challengers were the formidable Christy O'Connor, Bob Charles and, waiting to pounce, Jack Nicklaus. Former winners Peter Thomson and Roberto De Vicenzo were also in close attendance.

By the fourth hole of the final round, Jacklin was a commanding five strokes ahead of the field; all but Charles, the great left-hander, had fallen away. Charles – who had won the 1963 British Open, the first one in which Jacklin had played – had pulled back to within two strokes of the leader by the time they reached the 13th where Jacklin, not wanting any delays, had repaired his rival's driver.

The lead was still two as they reached the 18th, a tight par-four of 389 yards, embroidered with bunkers and the scourge of many aspirants in past British Opens. Players like O'Connor, Eric Brown and Nicklaus had perished here,

❝ ... when I saw where the ball was lying, I thought "that's it". ❞

and common sense might have argued for safety.

Jacklin, though, had driven well all day, and it never really entered his mind to play safe with an iron or 3-wood, even after watching Charles drive dangerously close to one of the fairway bunkers.

"I remembered how many good players had lost the Championship here by making a six," Jacklin said, "but I

decided I would not be cautious. I drove the ball over the bunkers at the left and watched as it slid back into the middle of the fairway." Against the wind it flew, finally stopping 260 yards away. This was a shot of supreme skill and confidence, and even before the ball found the hole, it confirmed Jacklin as a worthy Champion.

There was, of course, still a job to do, but surely nothing could go wrong now. With 130 yards to the flag, Jacklin went straight for his 7-iron, a favored club. A controlled half-shot and the ball was there, just 12 feet from the hole. It was all over now. "I knew I'd won it after that shot," Jacklin said afterwards. "I had been telling myself not to think about winning, but when I saw where the ball was lying, I thought 'that's it'." The crowd were so excited that they surged forward even before Jacklin made his triumphant march toward the green, actually stamping on his foot and causing him to lose a shoe. Enthusiasm of this sort from the normally reserved home crowd had never been seen on a British course before.

With a two-stroke cushion and Charles, at best, in with a four, the confidence to go for the putt was there. Jacklin's putt was true and almost long enough: the ball breathed its last an inch from the lip. Tony walked up and tapped in the shortest putt to win an Open.

It had been 18 years since British golfing fans had last acclaimed a British winner of the British Open, when Max Faulkner had taken the trophy in 1951. Jacklin's win was more than merely personal, though: it initiated a renaissance in European golf.

N.D

The relief of victory for Tony Jacklin (left) came only after a hard moment at the 6th hole (page 136).

❝ As bold a golfer as ever lived, Hagen never backed off from a challenge. ❞

Walter Hagen on the final green at Brae Burn with his main rival, Mike Brady, among the onlookers.

Throwing away what he considered a great chance to win the US Open by topping an overly ambitious wood shot to the 14th hole of The Country Club, Brookline, in 1913, Walter Hagen had decided golf wasn't his game. He dreamed of a career in baseball. He seemed about to realize that dream the following winter.

A dapper man, with slick black hair like patent leather, who cared as much about his dress as his swing, Hagen worked as the professional at the Country Club of Rochester, in upstate New York. With the Club closed for the winter, he went to Florida, where he became friendly with Pat Moran, the manager of the Philadelphia Nationals. Moran allowed Hagen to pitch in a few practice games, and when the team broke camp, Hagen was left with the impression he would be given a thorough trial the next winter.

Hagen floated back to Rochester on a cloud, planning to work at the Club, and pitch semi-pro baseball. He hadn't intended to enter the 1914 US Open, but Ernest Willard, the publisher of the *Democrat and Chronicle*, the Rochester newspaper, felt Walter had done remarkably well in his first try and offered to pay his expenses to Midlothian, near Chicago, for the 1914 Championship. Hagen accepted the offer, shot 290 and won by one stroke over Chick Evans. He forgot about baseball.

Evans and Jerry Travers, both amateurs, won the next two Opens, and then the United States entered the First World War in April 1917. While some golf was being played – the US Open and the PGA Championships were suspended, but the Western Open was played in 1917 – most of it was for charities connected with the war. Hagen had married in January 1917 and was exempt from the military draft. He spent those two years playing exhibitions for war relief. When the war

At his peak, Hagen was the least graceful but most effective player of the era.

ended in November 1918, he was the best golfer in America and, except for the war years, he hadn't been without at least one title since 1913, even if it was of minor importance.

Never a picture swinger, he had learned to control a sway that had often sent his drives off in unpredictable directions, and while he had no equal from 100 yards in, he remained uncertain off the tee. Never one to mind, though, Hagen would shrug off a wild shot and work on the next, which he'd often drop close enough to the cup for a certain birdie. Without that knack he probably wouldn't have won the 1919 US Open, at the Brae Burn Country Club, near Boston, Massachusetts.

Walter played reasonably well through the first 54 holes, shooting 226, not a bad score for the times, but by then he had fallen five strokes behind Mike Brady, who seemed to have the Championship won. Mike stumbled round the last 18 holes in 80, however, finished with 301, then slumped into the clubhouse to wait.

Hagen heard of Brady's collapse standing on the 10th tee. Playing erratic

stuff himself, he would have to play the home nine in level par to match Brady.

His cause seemed lost when he hooked out-of-bounds on the 11th, but he made up for it with a birdie two holes later. One more and he would win.

He had his opportunity on the 18th, a strong hole with a stone wall close behind a green divided into two levels. A ball hit over the wall was out-of-bounds.

Hagen played a useful drive that left him within range with his second shot, but he would have to play a long iron to that scary green. Walter had no interest in second place; he played to win, but gauging this shot was not easy. He wanted the ball on the upper tier, toward the back, but the wall was so close that a slight miscalculation could cost him even a tie.

As bold a golfer as ever lived, Hagen never backed off from a challenge. He drew his mid-iron from his bag, the equivalent of a 2-iron, set himself, then drew it back with his usual slight sway, left knee cocked. He lashed the shot, timing the stroke perfectly.

The ball shot off a touch to the right of the flagstick, held its line, dropped on to the front level, then climbed the slope, stopping within eight feet of the cup. It was as courageous a shot as any man had played under those conditions and now Hagen could win the Championship outright, for no one holed as many critical putts.

Hagen also had a sense of the dramatic. He sent word ahead for Brady to come out of the clubhouse and watch him win. With Mike standing by, Walter stroked his ball straight for the hole. It caught the lip, then spun out. He finished with 75 and matched Brady's 301. There would be a play-off the next day.

Hagen shot 77, Brady 78. A man of lesser nerve wouldn't have been in the play-off at all.

R.S.

SEVE BALLESTEROS

*9-iron to the 16th at Royal Lytham and St Anne's
in the 1979 British Open*

S eve Ballesteros was 22 years old in 1979, a fresh-faced young Spaniard with an engaging smile, a classic golf swing and a burning will to win. He hadn't become the spiritual leader of Europe's revolt against American dominance of golf just yet, but he was on his way.

As a kid of 19 he had led the 1976 British Open after 36 holes and in the end tied Jack Nicklaus for second place, six strokes behind Johnny Miller, at Royal Birkdale. Later in the season he had helped Spain win the World Cup. A year after that he led the European Order of Merit, quite an accomplishment for a young man of 20.

Ballesteros, however, was not an ordinary young man. While he was

somewhat unreliable with his driver, he played inspired irons. Those who saw it will never forget the 2-iron he drilled to the heart of the 13th hole at the Wack Wack Golf Club in Manila during the 1977 World Cup, a piercing shot that covered the flagstick all the way and came to rest within 10 feet of the cup. He holed the putt for an eagle 3, and Spain was on its way to a second consecutive victory.

This was the kind of shot that brought to mind Byron Nelson and Ben Hogan, the two greatest iron players ever. Just as Nelson and Hogan had other qualities, so did Seve. If he wasn't the best escape artist of all the great players, he was close to it. He could find a way out of anything, creating the little chips and

Seve Ballesteros watches anxiously as his tee shot to the 16th in the final round heads towards the car park.

❦ *If he wasn't the best escape artist of all the great players, he was close to it.* ❧

pitches that made the difference between winning and losing.

He was also a superb craftsman on the green. He stroked the ball with a legato tempo and glorious touch, and although he used an unorthodox style, with the toe of his club raised slightly off the ground, he holed more critical putts than anybody. Michael Bonallack, the Secretary of the Royal and Ancient Golf Club of St Andrews, a man who had won five British Amateur Championships, called him "a fantastic reader of greens". Above all, he had a fiery temperament and he played the game with driving determination. Just as he was never out of a hole, he was never beaten until the last putt had been holed.

By 1979, however, he hadn't shown all those qualities. While he had been close to winning the 1976 British Open, he hadn't threatened in either of the next two. A weak 74–73 finish dropped him to 15th place, behind Tom Watson, in 1977, and a weaker 76–73 finish in 1978 earned him 17th place, behind Jack Nicklaus.

The 1979 British Open was played at Royal Lytham and St Anne's, on the western coast of England, about a mile inland from the Irish Sea. It is not among Britain's greatest courses, but it is certainly of Championship calibre, and its finish of six consecutive par four holes is as strong as any in the British Open rota.

As the last round began, Hale Irwin, the US Open Champion, led by two strokes over Ballesteros, but seven men were in position to win.

Playing as he had at Royal Birkdale, Ballesteros was straying off line with his drives, but saving himself with spectacular recoveries and confident putting. Still, he was behind, trailing the Australian Rodger Davis now, and he began the second nine by dropping one stroke at the 10th, then slicing his second shot badly on the 11th, a par five, and saving his par only by holing a 10-foot putt.

At the same time others were falling back, and when Ballesteros birdied the 13th, nearly driving the green, he had moved ahead. He played the next two holes in one over par, but even so picked up one stroke, and stood on the 16th tee with a two-stroke cushion.

It was nearly five o'clock then, on a sunny, breezy afternoon, with the wind fairly strong, crossing from left to right. Rather than fight the wind, Ballesteros started his drive straight down the middle. Carried by the breeze, the ball drifted to the right, came down in the rough at least 30 yards off the center of the fairway and among parked cars. He was allowed a free drop. Fortunately, the gallery had matted the grass flat and he had a decent lie.

The 16th is not a long hole, only 356 yards, and Seve had but a pitch left, partially into the wind, just what he wanted. From there he played a superb pitch to a difficult green that normally runs away from the shot. The ball rose into the wind, seemed to come straight down, hit and held, and then drew back toward the cup, stopping perhaps 20 feet away. Seve holed the putt for the three, and increased his lead to three strokes with two holes to play.

Still playing nervous golf, Ballesteros saved a par on the 17th by holing from 10 feet, drove into the rough again at the 18th, and from an impossible lie somehow reached the green and saved another par. He shot 70 for the round, and 283 for the 72 holes. Jack Nicklaus and Ben Crenshaw tied for second, three strokes behind, at 286.

It was here perhaps more than in any tournament until then that Ballesteros showed the fighting spirit that would not accept defeat. This was his first important victory. A year later he won the US Masters, and within the next few seasons grew into the finest player in the game.

R.S.

ACKNOWLEDGMENTS

No book of this nature can be done without help. We've had plenty, all of it valuable, all of it given willingly and enthusiastically. We are especially grateful to Kathryn Murphy and Martha Gay, of the Augusta National Golf Club, and to Bill Inglish, the demon statistician; Donald (Doc) Giffin, from Arnold Palmer's office; Furman Bisher, of the *Atlanta Journal*; Charley Yates, the former British Amateur Champion; and special thanks to Al Ludwick, of the *Augusta Chronicle*; Robert Macdonald, of New York, the publisher of *The Classics of Golf*, who often led us in the right direction; and to Janet Seagle, of the United States Golf Association, and Andrea Stern, who found us these wonderful pictures.

PICTURE CREDITS

Yours in Sport 7, 11, 42 left and right, 43, 54, 74, 75, 87, 91, 104 top and bottom, 116, 116–117, 118, 124–125, 131

Peter Dazeley 9, 13, 14, 15, 16 top, 49, 70 bottom, 129, 143

Frank Christian Studio 12 top and bottom, 123

Colorsport 16 bottom, 38 top and bottom, 50 right, 70 top, 98, 99

Michael Hobbs Collection 17, 19, 26 top, 34 left, 44 left, 57, 89, 113

Phil Sheldon 18, 30 top and bottom, 47, 55, 58, 69, 71, 86, 88, 130, 141

Brian Morgan Golf Photography 21, 50 left, 53, 64 top, 66, 85 left, 94, 100

Associated Press 22 left and right, 39, 76–77, 102, 107, 119, 120–121, 132–133

Hulton Picture Library/Bettman Archive 23

United States Golf Association 24, 26 bottom, 32 top, 33, 34–35, 40 bottom, 45, 46, 48, 60–61, 62, 67, 79, 84, 90, 92–93, 95 left, 96 top, 111, 112, 127, 138–139

Hulton Picture Company 25, 137, 140

New York Times Photos/Golf World 28

AllSport 10, 29, 31, 32 bottom, 36, 52, 59 top and bottom (bottom Dave Cannon), 78, 80, 85 right (Budd Symes), 95 right (Dave Cannon), 97, 108, 128

Courtesy of Golf World 44 right, 56, 64 bottom

Glasgow Herald 51, 63, 105, 122, 134

Popperfoto 65

Sidney Harris/Golf World 40 top left and right, 101

Dick Severino, Golf Features Service 81, 82

International News Photos, Los Angeles, courtesy of Golf World 83

Chuck Brenkus 83 right

Bettman News Photos 96 bottom

Bob Thomas, Sports Photography 109, 110

Sportsphoto Agency/Stewart Kendall 114, 115

Sport and General/Golf World 135, 136

Bob Toski 72, 73